Moment
to Moment
The Transformative Power of Everyday Life

AMY SANDER MONTANEZ

Morehouse Publishing
NEW YORK · HARRISBURG · DENVER

Copyright © 2013 by Amy Sander Montanez

All rights reserved. No part of this book may be reproduced, stored in a retrieval system, or transmitted in any form or by any means, electronic or mechanical, including photocopying, recording, or otherwise, without the written permission of the publisher.

Unless otherwise noted, the Scripture quotations contained herein are from the New Revised Standard Version Bible, copyright © 1989 by the Division of Christian Education of the National Council of Churches of Christ in the U.S.A. Used by permission. All rights reserved.

Morehouse Publishing, 4775 Linglestown Road, Harrisburg, PA 17112

Morehouse Publishing, 19 East 34th Street, New York, NY 10016

Morehouse Publishing is an imprint of Church Publishing Incorporated.
www.churchpublishing.org

Cover art, *Night Swimming*, by Roger Hutchison
Cover design by Laurie Klein Westhafer
Typeset by Rose Design

Library of Congress Cataloging-in-Publication Data

A catalog record for this book is available from the Library of Congress.

ISBN-13: 978-0-8192-2879-6 (pbk.)
ISBN-13: 978-0-8192-2880-2 (ebook)

Printed in the United States of America

Contents

This book is dedicated to my mother, Jane Caroline Sharpe Sander (1924–2001). Her commitment to her psycho-spiritual journey set an example that encouraged me to start on my own path. From the Other Side, I believe she is still trying to show me the way and is cheering me on.

And to my father, William Anthony Sander (1922–), who continues to have a willing heart and curious mind. His belief in the importance of family and community has shaped many more lives than he can imagine.

Acknowledgments

I have been loved into being who I am right now by many people and circumstances in my life. From my first memories, those of my parents, siblings, home, my neighbors in Melville, New York, and St. Luke's Lutheran Church in Farmingdale, New York, I have been learning about love, hospitality, and living in community.

When I left home, I found another nurturing community at Furman University, where professors opened home and heart to me, where I was challenged to question the known and explore the unknown, and through the Collegiate Educational Service Corps (CESC), to reach out to those in the community who needed me. It was at Furman University that Doctor L.D. Johnson, the Baptist chaplain, took my husband, Nick, and me to our first Episcopal church. There, the Reverend Bob Riegel mentored us into becoming mature adults in a faith community. In many ways, because of Bob's guidance, we continue to believe in the power of faith communities.

During this time I had a formative professional experience at Wren Middle School, where fellow teachers and I encouraged each other in our vocations and our avocations. To this day I am grateful for those colleagues and for the students who trusted me with their lives and their minds. I remember you all and think of you often.

There are friends, mentors, and teachers in my field of marriage and family therapy as well. Russ Haber, Laura Dodson, Al

Pesso, Maurizio Andolfi, Salvadore Minuchin, and the late Carl Whitaker have each helped form who I am and how I practice the art of psychotherapy.

To my spiritual director's training program, Sursum Corda, I owe a debt of gratitude, and especially to the Reverend Marilyn Ascarza, Doctor E. Glenn Hinson, and the late Shaun McCartey, S.T. Their love of God and especially their love of Mystery inspired me. They modeled for me how to sit with myself and others as we open to our divine right, a relationship with the True Self and the Holy Other.

Big thanks and big love to Peggy Van Antwerp Hill, Ph.D. who first asked me to write and then continued to ask, who read this manuscript several times and made helpful suggestions, and to Carrie Stepp Graves, my office administrator, friend, and all around helpmate, for sitting with three different versions of the manuscript and piecing it together for me. To Roger Hutchison, for suggesting that he take an early manuscript to a conference where he had access to some publishers, and also for his beautiful cover art. To Sharon Pearson, who in the gentlest way turned down my first manuscript and made reasonable and specific suggestions that would make it better. And to Sharon, again, for asking me to write for Church Publishing Inc. in another venue.

To Joan Castagnone, the kindest, most generous editor a first-time author could ask for. Thanks for asking for my manuscript and for loving it. Thanks especially for taking the time to get to know me and my style.

On the home front, my colleagues, soul sisters, and friends, Nancy Beaver, Salley Lesley, Barbara Austin, Rena McClendon, Carrie Graves, Rhea Merck, Bren Schell, my women's group, my writing group, Jan Valle, Paul Valle (thanks for the headshot), Mark and Julia Sibley-Jones, Annamarie Saliba Arens, Nancy Richards, Amy Heit, Dianne Mitchell, Debbie Bruner, Robert and

Mary Ward Wisnewski, Suzanne Taylor, and Louise Deahl, all of whom keep me honest, keep me grounded, and keep loving me.

For anyone whose story is in this book, those named and unnamed. And for all my clients and friends who open their lives to my trust, who allow me to accompany them on the most sacred journey, that of the Self. Special thanks to those in my clergy support groups, who in many ways anointed my gifts and encouraged me not to play small. I cannot name you all, but you know who you are and you know how precious you are to me.

To my dad, William Anthony Sander, and to my siblings and their spouses, Jean and Jack, Alan and Fran, Eric and Loretta. Thank you for believing with me in the importance of family, for keeping me humble, for reminding me often of my faults and weirdnesses, and also for seeing my gifts and affirming them.

And always, to my daughter and Zen master, Maria Christine, and my husband and love, Nick, whose own journeys have gracefully intersected with mine. Thank you for believing in me and wanting me to live a vocational life. Sometimes I love you more than it feels my heart can hold.

A Spiritual Friend and Companion for You

E. Glenn Hinson

Thomas Merton challenged us to practice contemplation in a world of action. A friend labeled him "a contemplative at the heart of the world." That phrase recognized that, although he pursued his calling to a life of prayer in a monastery, Merton took the world into his heart and addressed some of its problems with deep insight and searching concern.

Where this great spiritual master brought insights from the contemplatives to bear on the world we live in from his hermitage, Amy Montanez, a licensed professional counselor, marriage and family therapist, and spiritual director, takes us with her into her "world of action" and shows us how to be attentive to "the Beyond in our midst." To use her own phrasing, she introduces us to "the transformative power of everyday life."

You can't read far into this small book before you realize that you are a companion of a skillful counselor and a wise spiritual friend, deeply in love with God, with others, and with the whole creation. You feel like she is right there talking to you, sharing from authentic experience informed by years and years of study and reflection.

As I read *Moment to Moment*, I realized that I would not get the full benefit of this spiritual companionship by reading straight through, although doing that furnished me with a lot of "aha!" and "yes, yes!" moments. No, I would gain the most by meeting with the author once a day or once a week for a year or however long it would take to go chapter by chapter to the end—like meeting with a counselor or a spiritual director. During that day or week, I would put what I was learning to the test, letting these ideas whirl around in my heart and mind to see how they worked. And they will work. People must have done something like that when they came to Jesus or the desert fathers and mothers seeking spiritual counsel.

Each chapter, you will see, has a set of questions appended. They are searching questions, not easily answered. They are the kind of queries not just a teacher but, even more, a loving spiritual companion might put to you. They bring to my mind the questions Jesus raised of the two disciples who walked with him on the way to Emmaus (Luke 24:13–35). Just like those disciples, no matter how much we ponder the questions, we may not catch on during the whole journey until we come to "the breaking of bread."

Amy Montanez's meditations reveal amazing breadth. She, of course, is expertly outfitted in psychology and psychotherapy. But what impresses me more is an expansive ecumenism that is rooted in the Lutheran heritage of her parents but extends far beyond to the Episcopal Church, Roman Catholic Church, Judaism, Buddhism, and other great religious traditions. And there's depth, not just depth in psychology but in the way she draws from these many sources of wisdom to carry on these conversations with you.

Spend some time with Amy Montanez, and you will discover a way to achieve what Christians have sought to do all through their history—to pray without ceasing. Another way to think about it is to make all of life a prayer, attentive to God in everything you do. This book can change your life.

Introduction

I crawled into bed, pulled the covers up, and began praying. "Please, God, don't send another horrible dream tonight. I don't understand them. I am trying and obviously failing to figure them out. But I am exhausted from the dreams. Please let me sleep soundly tonight." I prayed this prayer the night before my first appointment with a new spiritual director. I had picked someone who was a licensed professional counselor, a priest, and a person I knew to have extensive training in dream work. I needed serious help. My dream life was unsettling me to the point I no longer wanted to go to sleep.

After several sessions, the dreams, which felt more like nightmares to me, stopped. The key, as I understand it now, was hearing someone else affirm my natural and most comfortable way of being in the world—intuitive, gut-centered, private—and giving me permission to *choose* when I wanted to be the way the world pulled on me to be—analytical, head-centered, public. This was almost twenty years ago.

Much of my life's journey before and after that disturbing dream series has seemed haphazard. Unplanned. Unexpected. Random. In the moment. I have come to attribute this to the way I have relied on my gut feelings and intuition more than on my cognitive abilities and analysis. I am bright enough. Testing shows that I am whole-brained, balanced, and capable of both creativity and analysis. But mostly it is my intuition and deep gut feelings that guide me. Because of this, much of what I do looks and sometimes feels like an afterthought. I left high school a year early, not really knowing why; I just *felt* it was time to go. I was done there. I went from Long Island, New York, to a small liberal arts college in Greenville, South Carolina, because I liked the way I *felt* when I visited there. While at college I could have majored in music, theatre, dance, or biology, but I *sensed* that it was better to go in the direction of education and psychology, my major and minor. As a middle-school teacher, I found myself informally counseling many students during lunch and after school, which led me to start my master's degree in Educational Counseling.

Once a school counselor, I began working with many families because . . . well . . . it just made *sense* not to work with children in a vacuum. This led me to seek out graduate courses and licensure in marriage and family counseling. I continued working with families in the schools until I *felt* like I should go into private practice. In private practice, I began asking clients, both individual and couples, how their faith lives affected their psychological journeys and healing, because I *intuited* that I was missing something by not asking that question. The more I did this, the more I *felt that* the next step of my journey should be to study spiritual direction.

During this training, I began practicing yoga because my body seemed to want a way to pray and integrate what I was *experiencing*. I soon began designing a curriculum for spiritual directors' training that included an integrated approach to psychological and spiritual healing and wholeness, and I began teaching that program. So, in my experience I find that I am already doing something or am aware of something from my intuition, and then I put some shape on it.

How did I start writing? Peggy Van Antwerp Hill, Ph.D., the former communications director of the Episcopal Diocese of Upper South Carolina and a friend of mine, asked me to do a couple of pieces for a publication entitled *Crosswalk,* an award-winning magazine of the Diocese of Upper South Carolina. One piece was on spiritual direction and another on Sabbath. The next year, she asked if I would like to write a regular column for the e-newsletter of the same diocese, one that would go out every two weeks. No pressure. She just invited me to give it a try. I certainly didn't fancy myself a writer, but I *felt* like I wanted to write about my own effort to live a courageous, whole-hearted life, one open to and aware of the present moment. So I began writing a bi-weekly column.

For three years I was faithful to this effort, and in the process I had many people tell me that my writing was speaking to them. They, too, could relate to the effort to stay present, take notice, watch, and wait. I heard often the comment, "You should write a book," and other than returning a weak smile and a thank you, I thought nothing of it. "I have a busy practice of therapy, spiritual direction, retreat leading, and teaching. Who has time to write a book? I would never be able to plan for that to happen," my inner dialogue quickly contained my anxiety.

On a two-week Sabbath in the mountains of North Carolina, I made the decision to reread all that I had written. I needed to remind myself what I had been about during the past few years and to listen to God's voice in the midst of all of that. It was in the rereading that I came to this realization; I write about just a few topics, and those topics, in many ways, are about the practice of trying to stay present and aware. I started sorting my articles into piles: inner work, everyday encounters, worship, community, Sabbath, vocation. Finally, I could *sense* the shape of a book. "Oh, now I understand. This *could* be a book. I see the shape of it now. And maybe it would be a book that would help others on their journeys to stay present and aware." For me, it was an important moment. When I told friends, family, and colleagues about it, they smiled and some smirked. They had been trying to encourage me in this for years.

So here it is. My book. A book about transformation—spiritual, life-changing transformation available to you in the life you are living right now. It is a compilation of personal essays divided into sections that reflect and explore the ways in which we experience the transformative process.

I begin each section by offering a framework and context for the pieces that follow. Some of them teach overtly. Others embody the transformative process in a more experiential style. At the end of each piece is a section entitled, "Digging Deeper." These questions are designed to help you reflect honestly about yourself, and then consider how to be your most authentic self in community. Back and forth, from inner reflection to sharing with others, these questions should help you consider not only the personal level but also the relational/community level of your journey. The infinity sign on each page is a reminder that we move from one to the other in the transformative process.

My hope is that the book will be an encouragement for you as you look at your own life. No need for gurus. No secret technique. Just slow down. The path is already there. Pay attention to the daily promptings of the Holy Spirit. Encounter others with awareness. Watch for the thread that weaves the randomness of your life into a beautiful tapestry. Embrace yourself in all of your humanity. Be compassionate to yourself and others. Mostly, be who you are most authentically.

If you are using this book with a group, my prayer is that you will create a safe space together and encourage each other to be present to the moment, notice the constant presence of the Holy, and connect with each other in a compassionate and vulnerable way. Allow the Holy Spirit to transform you and you will then transform the world.

I.

INNER WORK IS GOD'S WORK:

TRANSFORMED FROM WITHIN

Start close in,
Don't take the second step
Or the third,
Start with the first
Thing
Close in,
The step you don't want to take.

—David Whyte[1]

Dr. Charles Brewer was one of those professors that students loved and feared. I felt both privileged and punished taking his Experimental Psychology class while attending Furman University from 1974–1978. His tests were known to stump even the brightest students, and his lectures were animated but dense. Students were alternately laughing at his antics or panicking about the material being presented.

I showed up one day with a particularly malnourished imagination, having been up most of the night working on an experiment that involved rats and conditioning. I have no idea what question I asked, but after Dr. Brewer answered it, he walked over to my desk, stood within inches of me, stared down his very straight, thin nose, looked through me with his intense eyes, and delivered his famous saying, "Everything is related to everything else, dammit Ms. Sander, and don't you ever forget it."

Somehow this statement began to worm its way into my heart and mind. As my journey with spirituality and psychology continued, I came to believe that spirituality and psychology are intimately connected. Good spirituality is innately therapeutic. The experience of God, felt, lived, and embraced should, indeed, heal us. Good psychology, depth psychology, should not be restricted to solving problems of daily living, but should also be attending to the unique soul of the individual. So related are these two disciplines that I imagine them like a double helix DNA molecule, one thread informing the other until there is no artificial divide, no turf war. These disciplines have evolved beyond the dualism of the Renaissance and the Enlightenment, and we know now that we can allow for a personal, mystical experience of the Holy, at the same time believing in the scientific knowledge we have of the human psyche.

My personal/professional work as a therapist and spiritual director has only affirmed this belief. I have, from my professional beginnings, had the dissonant experience of trying to separate these two fields. Why? Because my therapy clients who were willing to explore their spiritual beliefs healed more quickly and reported experiences of transformation. Those seeing me for spiritual direction expressed a greater sense of wholeness and healing when they allowed their psychological work and wounding to enter into the process.

Over time I added one more thread to the helix, the body. That sacred place where our psyches, souls, hearts, and minds are housed, our bodies don't lie. They store memories and experiences, and paying attention to our bodies can often lead us to our own truths. Sometimes on the journey of transformation, we have to focus on one thread at a time, as if untangling this triple helix. We look at the psyche, the spirit, and the body separately, not because they *are* separate, but because it makes dealing with a complex system manageable when we do. The deep healing comes, though, when we start to integrate body, mind, and spirit. It doesn't matter which thread—body, mind, or spirit—we start with first. In the end, we weave the pieces back together into a beautiful helical creation, stronger now with each strand healed.

This process of healing and being healed, of living into our uniqueness and fullness, is, to me, the greatest joy in life. We are all trying to find our way back Home, home to our holy nature, and this is how we do it, healing thread by thread. I believe this kind of personal transformation requires three things of us: courage, perseverance, and community.

Courage, because one of the hardest things we do as people who believe in transformation is to look at the truth of ourselves. Being vulnerable and truthful with ourselves, God, and others is courageous work. Sometimes the process of this inner work, the process of claiming our personal truths can feel negative, dark, and full of grief. For some of us, it is even scary to look at our light and our strengths. Somehow we know that our lives will change if we claim and share our stories and our personal truths. We also know that we can't control how they will change, and giving up that control can be frightening. It can also be freeing.

That is why perseverance is necessary. Transformation is not an easy process and there is no quick fix. Changing any system is always difficult, and changing our inner system might be the most difficult change of all. I credit my mother with helping me at a young age begin to understand the process of transformation. Her symbol for transformation was the butterfly. Every imaginable presentation of butterflies adorned our house—paintings, sun-catchers, napkins, bathroom wallpaper and towels, figurines, tchotchkes, clothing, jewelry, and tote-bags. And though the beauty and color of butterflies surrounded me in my home, I learned that the process of becoming one was not easy. I watched this happen one time when I was in grade school and I had a terrarium in my bedroom. Inside the terrarium was a caterpillar cocoon on a stick. I awoke one morning to see the tip of a wing sticking out of the cocoon. When I came home from school that day and raced up the stairs to my bedroom, just a fraction more of the black wing was visible. "Mom, why is this taking so long?" I yelled. She came up to my room. I still remember what she said to me. "Becoming a completely new creature is slow work, Amy. Maybe the butterfly is tired and needs a break. Don't worry. The butterfly knows that it was meant to be a butterfly, and it will continue to come out of that cocoon when it is ready. It will persevere." And like the butterfly, sticking with the process and believing we are worth it, we will come out transformed into our own unique Self.

In the two decades that I have worked with the transformative process, the aspect that seems the hardest for some of us is belonging to and participating in community. Most of us need support and encouragement, so having a sense that we are not in this process of transformation alone can go a long way in helping us stay on the path. However, honest community makes us vulnerable and open, so the possibility to be hurt again is very real. Because it is in relationship that we get hurt, it is also in relationship that we heal, practice transformation, and see the fruits of our psycho/ spiritual labor. The paradox of risk and reward is truly felt when we decide to enter into any honest relationship. That's simply the truth. You might get hurt. *And*, you might get healed. You have to weigh the risk. When I do, I always come out on the side of community and relationship. For some, a faith community is the answer. For others, a support group like a 12-Step group is the answer. Groups that form around similar interests like women's groups, men's groups, Bible studies, book clubs, dream groups, and writing groups can become healing communities.

For some of us, becoming vulnerable, honest, and open to the quiet and loving support of friends and family may be all that is necessary. In whatever way we decide to engage in community, all we have to do is start, take that first step, and the Holy One will be there, supporting and guiding our efforts. A community relationship becomes transformative when it is lived as a sacrament, "an outward and visible sign of an inward and spiritual grace" (The Book of Common Prayer, 857).

Experience has taught me that inner work and the transformative process are well worth the effort. Perhaps you could find guidance in a therapist, spiritual teacher, soul friend, or safe group. Use all the trusted resources you can find. Learning a contemplative form of prayer, sometimes called meditation, has been an indispensable part of the process for me and many others. Finding a way to still our minds and connect with the Holy One is an experience that can positively change our perception of ourselves and the world.

Dr. Brewer was a brilliant psychologist and passionate educator. What I think he might not have realized was that he was a spiritual mystic. Everything is related to everything else. In our earthly form, we are a miraculous helical creation, differing threads woven together to make a perfect whole. And dammit, don't you ever forget it.

Ready?

Do you want to be healed?
—John 5:6 (RSV)

When the student is ready, the student will see the teacher.
—Peggy Van Antwerp Hill, PhD[2]

In my childhood home, whenever we were getting ready to go somewhere, anywhere, to church, on vacation, to a party, or out for a visit, my mother would say, "I'm ready," and my father would walk out the door and start the car. If the kids were going along, we would follow. This would start the inevitable tension. After a few minutes, my father would start honking the horn, saying things like, "Where is your mother? She said she was ready." Sometimes he would send one of us in to "check on her," which really meant to hurry her along.

"I'm ready," to my mother, meant that she was in her slip with her jewelry on, and that she would, momentarily, put on her dress, change her purse, shut out the lights, check on the pets, lower the thermostat, put on her coat, apply her lipstick, and then walk out the door. By the time she appeared, my father would be frustrated, silent, and angry.

Sometime in the 1980s I laughed my way through a magazine article while waiting at a doctor's office. Written by a clever author, whose name I cannot remember, the article talked about stages of readiness. There was *"ready,"* which in my life was my mother in her slip and jewelry. Then there was *"really ready,"* which translates to my mother dressed and now changing her purse. There was "*ultra-ready*," which would have been my mother coming down the stairs, checking on the pets, shutting out lights, and lowering the thermostat, and then there was "*supremely ready*," which in my life would have been my mother walking out the door. She usually ended up putting her lipstick on in the car. After reading the magazine article, I was excited to have a model to offer my extended family for dealing with our "readiness" drama. We now refer to it whenever we are together and issues around getting "ready" come up.

You can imagine my laughter when, on a recent Sunday morning getting ready to leave for church, I said to my husband, "It's 8:30, we need to be heading for the car," and he said from the closet, wearing only his underwear and socks, "I'm ready."

He knows the family joke. He's lived with my extended family on vacations and reunions. He's heard us all say, "OK, what stage of readiness are we in? Are we just ready or are we supremely ready?" He's heard us all say to my dad, "Sit down and relax, Dad. She's only ready, not even ultra-ready. Three more stages to go."

When I heard my husband say, "I'm ready" this past Sunday, not only did we both start laughing, but by the time I was sitting in church I began to associate those two words with spiritual readiness as well. What does it mean to be ready for the Divine to enter our lives? Are we ready, in our underwear and socks (metaphorically, of course), or are we supremely ready, walking out the door, truly starting the journey? I am reminded of the paralytic man by the pool called Bethsaida in John 5:5–14. He had been waiting at the healing pool for thirty-eight years, saying he wanted to be healed. It is clear to me now that he was not supremely ready. He may have been ready, like my mother in her slip. But until Jesus asked him if he wanted to be healed, he didn't move into a ready-er state. He wasn't supremely ready until the teacher came, and then his transformation moved right along.

What's the point of saying we're ready when we're really not anyway? Why not say, "I won't be ready for ten more minutes?"

Perhaps we want others to be happy with us, hoping we can fool them and keep them satisfied if we fudge on reality a bit. But if we only pretend we are ready for a relationship with God, who are we fooling? Surely not the Holy One.

God is waiting. At whatever stage of readiness we are, we can begin our journeys, without the need to manipulate or pretend. God will take us right where we are and accompany us from start to finish.

DIGGING DEEPER

1. What are your own stages of psycho-spiritual readiness?
2. When do you say you are ready when you really aren't? Why do you think you do this?
3. How do you distract yourself so that you are never really ready?
4. Some people have to experience a major crisis to undertake their inner work. What events, large or small, have drawn you into doing inner work?
5. Think about some psycho/spiritual disciplines that might help you be more ready to explore. For example, how do you think a daily devotional/meditation would help your stage of readiness? How could a relationship with a spiritual director or therapist be helpful to you? A prayer group? Would you be willing to be accountable to someone or a group for your spiritual journey?

Awakening from a Dream

*I have dreamt in my life, dreams that have stayed with me ever after,
and changed my ideas; they have gone through and through me, like
wine through water, and altered the color of my mind.*
—Emily Brontë[3]

*They say dreams are the windows of the soul—take a peek and you can
see the inner workings, the nuts and bolts.*
—Henry Bromel[4]

"Open your eyes. Take a deep breath. Sit up. You're dreaming," I
told myself over and over. Awakening from dreams, the ones that
you feel so deeply in your body you are sure they are happening, is
a precarious act. My dream, my unconscious, was pulling me back
in. I, my waking self, wanted to get out. It was an uncomfortable
tension. This particular dream was disturbing and I was troubled
upon awakening. My heart was beating quickly and my breathing
was shallow and quick. I was sweating and wasn't quite sure where
I was. I wanted to shake it off, to get out of it. Yet I knew it was
trying to tell me something, probably something I did not want to
hear and something I did not already know. Because I believe that
all dreams come to us in the service of our wholeness and healing,
I was able to give myself over to the dream for a few more minutes. I did finally sit up in bed, encouraging myself to breathe, to
pray, to ask the Holy for guidance as I opened myself to the possibilities of the dream message.

This dream, I believe, was taking me back about thirty years. I
was being asked to consider, to reconsider, the meaning of certain

events from that time in my life. New light was being shed three decades later. I was being asked to do another layer of emotional work and to allow for new healing. The vulnerability I was feeling left me weak and scared. I wanted my husband, who was out of town, and a girlfriend, who lives in another city, to hold me. Sitting with this alone was not fun; still I think it was meant to be. I needed the time to turn to God only, with all of my fears, and to let the Holy Mystery soothe me.

Why am I dreaming this? What do these symbols mean? Who is this person in the dream? How is it that this stirs me so deeply? As I held all of these questions up in prayer, the possibilities began to unfold. Events in a friend's life—a difficult and toxic relationship—were triggering memories from a similar relationship in my earlier life. God knew I needed another look at all of that. I needed to look more deeply into my role in that earlier relationship. God, through this dream, provided me with a new lens. It didn't feel good. Still doesn't. I thought I was done with all of this.

There's a saying, "If you want to make God laugh, tell him your plans." I heard myself chuckle. "Okay, God. You win. I am not done with this and you are not done with me. You want me to be healed from the inside out. That light you are shedding is a little startling, though. I am squinting at best. A little dimmer, a little slower would be better. I promise to hang in there. The dream has convinced me. I believe you are with me."

Healing can be slow, confusing, frightening, or thrilling. However it happens, it rarely happens all at once. We revisit our wounds in our life, time and time again, and discover new layers of God's grace and mercy, new layers of healing. It might hurt. It might be scary. My mother used to say, "Being responsible is not for the faint of heart." She was right, and I believe the healing journey is worth it.

DIGGING DEEPER

1. Think about a startling dream you've had. What new perceptions might it be trying to show you in the service of your healing and wholeness? How can you treat this or any dream as if it is a message from the Holy One to aid you in your spiritual life? Begin to honor your dreams by writing them down in a dream journal.

2. Most dreams come to show us something we don't already know. Each part/person/object/geographic location might be a representation of the dreamer's self. Take just one aspect of the dream and let yourself wonder about it? Ask yourself, "What part of me might be represented by that?"

3. Sometimes the events of a day or week trigger a dream. Ask yourself, "What was going on in my life the day that I had this dream? Was there a conversation? A book I was reading? A recent event in the news? Events in a friend's life?"

4. Sometimes it takes courage to look at your dream. Write about the fears you are being asked to face. Would it help to process this dream with a group of friends or a dream group? Community can be very supportive and encouraging in understanding our inner lives.

5. Is there another possible way that in God's sovereignty your wounds might be used for good? Is there another piece of your story that needs to be surrendered to the Great Healer? How might your past wounds be of use to a community or a relationship?

Deception

Telling the truth in a culture of deceit and lies is exhausting but ultimately healing work. We need the honest Great Physician, even if he tells us things we don't want to hear.
—Frank Honeycutt[5]

No one can persuade another to change. Each of us guards a gate of change that can only be opened from the inside. We cannot open the gate of another, either by agreement or by emotional appeal.
— Marilyn Ferguson[6]

Like an Oxford shirt off the dry cleaner's press, the sky was blue and crisp. The sun seemed to shine straight down to earth, no clouds in sight to filter or soften its brilliance. The leaves were motionless. From the kitchen window, the day seemed to beckon me: "Come out and play. Come out and play."

"Seventeen degrees," my husband called from the bedroom where he was checking The Weather Channel for the most recent update. "It's a deceptive day."

"Ah, deception," I thought. Things are not always as they seem, or how we wish they were. Not even in nature. What a hard lesson for us to learn.

I struggle with the issue of deception, having had a hard time losing my naïveté in life. I'm good with the obvious. I wasn't blown away by the greed on Wall Street or the scandals in the government. I am never surprised by the mishaps or moral lapses in character committed by celebrities or people in positions of power. Disappointed often, but not surprised. I paid attention in history class and I've read enough to suspect that people in power and people with money are exponentially more exposed to temptation than the average citizen. I am sure Jesus spoke about money so much because it alone must cause more temptation than anything else we encounter.

Often people who come to me for therapy or spiritual direction will, when comfortable enough, use the words, "You might find this hard to believe but . . . ," and I generally sit quietly, realizing that the person is more surprised by their own behavior than I am. Although every story has its own uniqueness and its own specific need for healing and reconciliation, the themes are often similar. Lying. Cheating. Shame. Addictions. Anger. Abuse. Sexuality concerns. Whatever the issue, the truth is *we* find it hard to believe when we've done something we think we're not capable of. It surprises *us*. "I find this hard to believe about myself" is probably the more accurate statement. We've deceived ourselves and in doing so have deceived others. We've turned a blind eye to what we don't want to know about ourselves. In therapeutic terms, we call this the shadow, that part of ourselves from which we are alienated.

"I've followed too much the devices and desires of my own heart" (The Book of Common Prayer, 62), we say in corporate confession. It is an appropriate confession, although I do believe it addresses only half of the paradox. I believe that in our heart of hearts, that place where the God-seed is planted in us, what we want for ourselves is exactly what the Holy One wants for us. Those desires were put there at our creation. So, there is a True Heart, the one given to us by God, and a Lived Heart, a place where the emotions and desires that have come from living and being hurt reside. It is to the Lived Heart that we must look to examine those devices and desires. If we stopped deceiving ourselves, perhaps things could be different. It's a spiritual discipline to pay attention to the shadow. It is hard work, work we'd rather

not do sometimes. We can actively and knowingly deceive ourselves and others; we can also do it passively and turn a blind eye.
We can choose to stay unconscious and unaware.

Hardest for me, it seems, is the jolt I feel when someone I
know and love deceives me. "How could this be?" I find myself
naïvely saying, as if I don't know that we're all, myself included,
capable of deception, active and passive. It always stings. My opti-
mism and theological belief that we are all carrying the image of
Christ keep me expecting the best of myself and of others. And
so I have to decide what to do when someone deceives me. Is this
something worth a conversation? A confrontation? Or is this one
of those things I should let pass with a mental note to be more
aware? How do I stay connected and in relationship while paying
attention to what is real and possible? No wonder authentic, intimate relationships are such hard work. Being honest with yourself
and then being honest with another is a lifetime of effort. This
kind of honesty, vulnerability, and intimacy is the work of the sacramental and transformative relationship.

True friendships, those relationships where we can speak
the truth, especially about ourselves, can lessen the possibility
of our being subject to our own deception. When we feel comfortable enough with another person, we can offer up thoughts
about the parts of ourselves we'd rather forget. We can say things
that make us vulnerable and reveal our deep imperfection. We
can know that it is in those times of acknowledging our human-
ness and imperfections and have them accepted with warmth and
empathy that we can truly be open to radical transformation.
True friendship is healing.

Hearing these words from the Psalter recently, I was struck
again with another important truth.

> For God alone, my soul in silence waits. . . .
> Truly, my hope is in him.

He alone is my rock and my salvation,
my stronghold so that I shall not be shaken. . . .
Those of high degree are but a fleeting breath,
Even those of low estate cannot be trusted. . . .
Put no trust in extortion; in robbery take no empty pride;
Though wealth increase, set not your heart upon it.
   (Psalm 62)

It is my intention to strive always to be authentic and trust-worthy, and I have friends that share this priority. But we are not God, and we will stumble and fall. And from those falls, we are called to learn more and be refined further into the image of God. H. A. Williams, the Anglican theologian, has said, "The opposite of sin can only be faith, and never virtue." I agree. We cannot will ourselves to perfection. Ultimately, we can only turn ourselves and those we love over to the Refiner's fire. We do that by acknowl-edging all the ways we are capable of deceiving ourselves and oth-ers. We acknowledge that by being faithful to our inner work and spiritual journey. We have the courage to remain faithful in our human relationships by staying faithful in our relationship with the Holy One.

DIGGING DEEPER

1. What is the hardest quality for you to accept in yourself? How is it affecting your personal healing and transformation?

2. Imagine having the courage to change something about yourself that you know needs changing? What would it take to have that courage? Think of a symbol or image of courage that you find helpful. Put that image in a handy place so that you can access it when you are fearful.

3. What are some works, maybe a Psalm or poem, that help you look at your own struggle with deception? It might be helpful for each member of a small group to share these.

4. With what friends or in what community are you able to be fully yourself, without a need for deceit or a mask? Name those people in your prayers. How do you protect the sanctity of these friendships and communities?

5. If, as H. A. Williams suggests, you cannot will yourself to a virtuous life, what does the process of transformation look like for you personally?

Jesus, The Great Receiver

It is better to give than to receive.
Jesus gave his life for us so that we may have eternal life.
Giving back to the world is the key to a well-lived life.
There are two kinds of people in the world: givers and takers.

I am in my mid-fifties now, and I have been well schooled in the statements listed above. I give in many different ways, as I'm sure you do, and I encourage others to do the same. Giving is modeled by Jesus, all the great saints, and all of my mentors. I give of myself for a living. I've walked a fine line of being "given out" because of the amount of giving (listening, caring, compassion, accommodating, care-taking, self-sacrificing, and huge investments of time) that is required in my personal and professional life at different times.

And so it was a great challenge for me when Mark Yaconelli, the keynote speaker at a retreat sponsored by "Companions on the Inner Way," asked us to consider Jesus as the "Great Receiver." If you want to know how to receive, Yaconelli suggested, look at Jesus. When a woman wants to pour expensive oil over his head he says, "Yes. How wonderful. I will receive this gift." When someone wants to wash his feet, he says, "What a beautiful act of kindness and comfort. Yes, please continue." When God opens the heavens and says, "You are my beloved Son with whom I am well pleased," Jesus says, "Yes. Yes. Yes. I will receive this affirmation."

How well do I receive? I can receive a compliment now, although I've had to work on being able to do that over the years.

I learned how to receive meals from others when my daughter had surgery. I love receiving a caring, thoughtful phone call or a gift.

If I keep on digging down, I have to ask myself, "How well do I receive the amazing gift of everyday life? What do I do with the gift of good health? In what ways do I fully receive the love of my family and friends?"

And more deeply, "Can I receive the gift of God's unconditional love for me? Do I really believe in the gift of my baptism, that I belong to a communion of saints and that I really am one of them? Can I acknowledge and receive the gifts God planted in me at my making and own them without apology or a need to make them less or different than they are? Do I believe that I am enough, just the way I am?"

The therapist in me knows how important it is for people to receive. When a child offers love to a parent and the parent cannot receive that love, it does great damage. Children need to know that their love matters, that their love reaches and influences their parents, that their parents are affected by the love that is given. After all, love is all a child has to give. The same is true in a partnership. If a partner cannot receive love that is being offered, the *energy* that we call *love* is thwarted and diminished.

Aging parents often have a hard time receiving love in the form of help. Pride gets in the way, and fear of losing independence, and so the parent deftly bats the love and help away. Love is a circuit much like electricity, and if either end of the circuit, the giving or the receiving end, is damaged, you have a short circuit. I know it is important to receive.

Naïvely, I had never thought about looking to Jesus as a model of receiving. I am now wondering about all the ways Jesus received the love of his earthly father and mother and about the ways he received the love of his followers. I am wondering what Jesus felt like when he received the affirmation and love of God. How did it transform him? When he went off to pray by himself, was it to receive? Did he, like I do, weaken at the knees when truly receiving the many forms of abundance that are offered in life?

How can I better receive the love of God? Can I believe that I am enough? I am playing with/praying with these questions as I think of Jesus as a model for receiving.

At the time of our Sunday offering we sometimes sing Hymn 424 in the Episcopal Hymnal. The words to verse three strike me now to be about receiving.

> For the harvests of the Spirit, thanks be to God.
> For the good we all inherit, thanks be to God.
> For the wonders that astound us,
> For the truths that still confound us,
> Most of all that love has found us,
> Thanks be to God.[7]

I will be praying with these ideas for many years. Receiving requires a softening, an allowing, an inviting. Can we believe that receiving is just as transformative as giving? Moment by moment, softening to this gift that is life, looking to Jesus as a model of receiving, I invite you to join me.

Digging Deeper

1. What is the unique way that you receive love? Another way to think about this is to ask yourself, "What is my favorite way of being loved?"

2. How would you describe the emotion you feel when you soften enough to receive the abundance in your life? Frequently, when we soften, we feel vulnerable. How would you explain the feeling of being vulnerable to someone else?

3. In what communities such as family, friends, clubs, church, and school are you most likely to feel like you are receiving love? How do those in your community know that you receive the love they offer? How do you let them know?

4. In what way could you make a commitment to pay attention to the way you receive what life offers?

5. Here is a practice suggestion: When you are feeling like there isn't enough, or like you aren't enough, take an intentional deep breath and allow yourself to imagine the feeling of abundance. Say to yourself: There is enough. I am enough.

Just Say Yes

Sometimes the only available transportation is a leap of faith.
—Margaret Shepard[8]

There is a vitality, a life force, an energy, a quickening that is translated through you into action, and because there is only one of you in all of time, this expression is unique. And if you block it, it will never exist through any other medium and it will be lost. The world will not have it. It is not your business to determine how good it is nor how valuable nor how it compares with other expressions. It is your business to keep it yours clearly and directly, to keep the channel open. You do not even have to believe in yourself or your work. You have to keep yourself open and aware to the urges that motivate you. Keep the channel open . . .
—Martha Graham[9]

Years ago I was motivated to start a theatre troupe in Columbia, South Carolina. It was called Theatre of Dreams and was structured after the NYC Theatre of Dreams, which I saw perform at the Spoleto Festival in Charleston, South Carolina. Bob Paton, the conceiver and director of the New York troupe, agreed to train a local group to be actors in this theatre. Our job was simple: to hear the nighttime dreams of audience participants and, by using improvisation, act out the dream as the dreamer watched.

Our first week of training mostly involved acting exercises. A cardinal rule of improv is, "Just say yes." When someone starts a motion, movement, or invitation, you are to receive it and keep the action going. In other words, if someone hands you a ball, you are to accept it and do something with it. If someone drapes an arm around you, you are to accept it and keep going. If someone calls you Bob, you are to go with that and not stop and say, "Wait, my name isn't Bob, it's Susie." Just say "yes" and that keeps the action moving.

Just saying yes, of course, has the potential to take us out of our comfort zones. I hadn't been planning on going in that direction. You couldn't mean me accepting that offer, could you? I don't know how to do that. I am not qualified/certified/trained/educated to do that. Wait, that's not right, you must have made a big mistake. You've got the wrong person.

Once, when I was a student at Furman University, the provost called me into his office and asked me if I would be interested in going to Japan to help start an exchange program. "Where? I am already signed up to go to Vienna and use all of my German language skills. Japan? Why me?" He said the faculty had specifically talked about why I would be a good candidate, something to do with my move from Long Island, New York to Greenville, South Carolina to attend Furman. "We figured you were already cross-cultural," I remember him saying. I do not remember why, but I said yes, then talked my parents into saying yes, and then lived five formative months in a country I would never have thought to visit. Being exposed to the Far East, to a culture much more ancient than that of the United States, to completely different religions and different social norms, and to the hospitable and gracious people I got to meet and live with in Japan, changed my life forever.

Several times in my life, trusted friends have dragged me out of my comfort zone. One time a friend called me and asked me to officiate over her wedding ceremony. Mary Anne, petite as she is, has a big free spirit and a strong streak of rebel in her. I should have known she wouldn't have a conventional wedding.

"I can't do that. You need an ordained minister," to which she quickly responded, "No I don't. You just need to be a notary and I will pay the $25 for you to become one. I want you to marry us."

The experience was memorable and affirming.

Another time a priest-friend of mine asked me to be one of the featured Lenten speakers at his church in another town. I am not practiced in the pulpit and I certainly felt like this would be out of my comfort zone. "Are you sure? I've never done anything like that before," I quickly countered. "I wouldn't be asking you if I wasn't sure" was the reply. I had a wonderful time and met lively and hospitable people. The Holy One used me in ways I never expected. The day was a grace and a blessing.

Yoga class often gives me an opportunity to try something that may be out of my comfort zone. It is so easy for the mind to say, "Oh no, I cannot do that. And not only can I not do it today, I will NEVER be able to do that." Perhaps that is true. Maybe we do have injuries or our personal body structure may limit our range of movement. It is certainly prudent to honor our bodies and not push them beyond where they can go. However, if it is possible just to hold a "yes" in the mind's imagination, then there is space to try, opportunities to get the ego, with all of its mighty holds, out of the way and open our bodies and our minds to new possibilities. My body can do things now it couldn't even imagine a decade ago.

Writing my first column for an e-publication was the result of a good friend offering me that venue. "I'm not sure," I wavered, excuse after excuse coming out of my mouth. "You know how full my client load is, and I've got that big retreat coming up in a few months. I have to finish my doctoral project, and I am trying to pack the house up so we can put it on the market." I was almost out of breath as I blabbered my excuse list to her listening ear. Calmly, she took all the stumbling blocks out of my way. The bi-weekly column took me way out of my comfort zone and started me on a writing path that continues and has led me to writing this book. The first writers' conference I attended was the result of a nudge and "just saying yes" to that nudge. That week at the

College of Preachers at the National Cathedral was a completely new experience. Being given the gift of hours every day to hunker down and write was in some ways stunning. "Oh, this is what it takes to really write," I thought as the week progressed. Hours and hours of silence. Gifted authors offering me feedback. More hours of writing and more feedback. My eyes and my imagination were opened in new and exciting ways through that process.

After winning the Super Bowl in 2010, New Orleans Saints Quarterback Drew Brees agreed to do a Dove for Men commercial. His acting debut involved taking a shower and being happy and spontaneous, free enough to sing in the shower. During an interview he said that the experience had pushed him right out of his comfort zone and that he had a great time. Why not? Just say yes.

I am not proposing some kind of co-dependent, addictive style of living in which we do not know our boundaries or our limitations. It is important to know when to say no and why we say no. It is important to understand our underlying motives and intentions and to be conscious of them. I am advocating for something very different, which is the paradoxical edge to proper boundaries and limits. When we are clear about our limits and boundaries, we are free, indeed, to say a holy "Yes" when we are offered the right opportunity. We are free to try new things in new ways and to trust in the process that the Holy Spirit designs for us. We are free to "just say yes" to God's nudgings.

The gospels are full of people who learn to "just say yes" to life. It may even be one of the underlying messages of scripture. Learn how to discern the promptings of the Spirit, listen for the voice of God, align with the image of holiness, and just say yes. Abraham and Sarah said yes. Samuel said yes. Mary said yes. Jesus said yes. The disciples said yes. The woman at the well learned to say yes after a lifetime of saying no, the disciples cast their nets one more time, a man was willing to be lowered through the roof of a house.

I am trying to learn to say more yeses. Will you join me?

DIGGING DEEPER

1. Write about a recent time when you stopped the flow of something by saying no. Was saying no truly the right/good thing for you, or were you saying no out of fear, laziness, comfort, or stubbornness? Any other reasons?

2. If you could be one hundred times more courageous than you are right now, what would you do or attempt to do? What yeses would you say?

3. Write about a time you said yes to something, even begrudgingly, and ended up having a wonderful time. How did this experience encourage you to say yes more often? How would you encourage a friend to accept an opportunity that might just be an amazing experience?

4. What is something you've been yearning to do that you could accomplish more easily if you had community working/playing/praying with you? Pray that God will help you find an opportunity to let it unfold.

5. Draw or paint a picture that expresses the energy of "Yes." Or, if you prefer to write, write about a time when you said yes because you had a group saying yes with you. How was that helpful?

Miracles and Life Abundant

I came that they may have life, and have it abundantly.
—John 10:10

I was waiting for the kind of solution where God reaches down and
touches you with his magic wand and all of a sudden I would be fixed,
like a broken toaster oven. But this was not the way it happened.
Instead, I got one angstrom better day by day.
—Anne Lamott[10]

It seems to me transformation comes in many guises, and any transformation is its own kind of miracle. When we think about miracles, we often think of Jesus and the ways in which he made something amazing happen very quickly, something someone wanted really badly, like a child being brought back to life, eyes being made to see again, or a wedding going off without embarrassment. Many of us pray for these kinds of miracles. Dear God, please take away my pain. Please, God, heal his body from the cancer. Jesus, please let there be a job opening for me this month so that I can earn enough money to pay the bills. We are familiar with this kind of prayer and this kind of miracle.

More often, in my line of work, I see another kind of miracle. It is the kind of miracle that unfolds slowly, sometimes so slowly we might not realize it is happening. Have you seen the images of a flower unfolding on The Nature Channel, time-enhanced so that you can watch it over a few seconds, even though it actually took a few days? Sort of like that. It is the kind of miracle that we humans co-create with God, by participating with the Divine

Presence and by aligning our wills with God's will. And then, even though it takes weeks or months or years, all of a sudden we see the whole picture, and by golly, we know that transformation has happened and it is a miracle.

I got to see one of these miracles unfold recently. A college-age student came to me for anxiety problems and relationship issues. He was visibly a mess when I began seeing him, his thick neck red with anxiety, his breathing shallow, his speech jittery, and his thoughts scattered and unfocused. But he was willing, eager even, to get his life on a different path. He told me that his father had stopped drinking about six years earlier and that the whole family was in recovery. Dad was in AA, Mom was going to Al-Anon, and here he was, trying to put the pieces together. It was good work, and during each session he worked hard to understand the coping skills he had learned as a child, the ways he was sabotaging himself, and what it would take to put himself on the right track. In his childhood he had learned to be a care-taker, to read the moods of everyone in the house except his own, and to exist beneath the radar screen. When he began dating, he chose women who had serious problems, and he began taking care of them. He loaned several money, he tried to help one stop cutting herself, he let one move in even though she was unable to contribute to the living situation. In ways he liked being the hero and savior. But it was taking a terrible toll, and he recently got suspended for a semester because he wrote a paper for one of his girlfriends so she wouldn't fail her class. The professor could tell it wasn't her writing and confronted her. She ratted him out and they both got suspended. In therapy he focused on learning who he was, and what he needed and wanted. He began to learn to take care of himself and to believe he was worthy of a mutual, reciprocal, and intimate relationship. He stopped his involvement with needy women and started to experiment with learning how to have a female friend. After about a year of work, he left talk therapy and joined an Al-Anon group, and that, he reported, was very helpful. I had also suggested that he get an opinion from a psychiatrist about medication, because his anxiety often got the best of him and he made decisions out of an anxious place rather than a centered one.

About a year later, when he came back to therapy, many more pieces were in place. We began to talk about his spiritual journey, about the ways he prayed and the ways he was able to let God into his life. His family life had improved tremendously. He had graduated and was offered a wonderful job in his field, in a city away from home. He was excited and ready to leave and try life on his own for a while. All the destructive relationships were over, and he was happy to be single and exploring his own life, no longer feeling desperate to have someone filling the emotional void. His face glowed as he talked about the peace he now had in his life.

"It's a miracle," I said, as I watched his heart swell with gratitude for the life he was living. "It is," he responded. "I never thought I could feel this way. I never thought my life would feel this rich and this full. I never thought my family would be able to sit around the dinner table and have a normal meal and normal conversation. It is a miracle."

This miracle took six years. It took much hard work. Each member of his family took responsibility for his or her own actions and chose to get well. He, at quite a young age, decided to get the help he needed to live differently. He was fortunate to have a good doctor who could help him with effective medicine. He and his parents began to take their journey with God seriously and to let God into the healing process. Everyone began to listen for a Higher Power more earnestly. This is the kind of miracle we "co-create" with God. We have to do our part, and we have to let God do God's part. And then it can all work and the transformation can unfold.

I believe in both kinds of miracles, the ones that are completely given to us and happen quickly, and the ones we have to co-create with the Holy Other. I've known both kinds in my own life. But it is the second kind of miracle that I see more frequently and that keeps me believing in the work I do and in the promises God makes to us.

"I came that they may have life, and have it abundantly" (John 10:10).

DIGGING DEEPER

1. When have you experienced a miracle in your life? Consider writing about it or sharing it with a group.

2. The Chinese symbol for the word "crisis" is the same symbol for the word "opportunity." Think about a crisis you are in or have been in. What are the opportunities hidden within the crisis? Name them if you can.

3. If you are stuck in a crisis, what is your theory about why you are stuck? Name any psycho-spiritual pain that you are afraid to face. Name that in prayer. Name it in a journal or to another. Are there any others close to you who are affected by a crisis? What do you think your role is with this other person? Are you being called to help? Hold? Wait?

4. Who in your life can you count on to support you during times of vulnerability and crisis? Name those people in a journal or in prayer. Ask that their presence in your life hold you and support you in your journey of transformation.

When Winter Comes

Every mile is two in winter.
—George Herbert[11]

Grace groweth best in winter.
—Samuel Rutherford[12]

At approximately 6:00 a.m., I routinely take my first cup of coffee with me to a "sitting spot" outside of the house. It will either be the front or the back porch, depending on my mood and the amount of dew left by the night air. But as many mornings as possible, I like to be outside for a cup of coffee and my morning meditation. Precious, my late cat, used to join me for his morning massage and cuddle time. Now Bailey, my latest feline affection-whore, finds me for that mandatory morning ritual.

Recently as I settled in, I noticed how cold I was, so I went back in for some socks and a blanket. It won't be long now, I thought, before I won't be able to sit outside for my morning routine, and the couch will become my home for the coldest mornings of the year. Winter will be here before I know it, I thought, with its long, dark nights and its colder, more austere days.

We all know the times of winter in our own souls. We are familiar with dark and difficult phases. Sometimes these wintry episodes explode on us. But other times there are warning signs that winter, with its darkness and its harshness, will arrive soon. Either way, there is no escaping these austere and challenging seasons. Fear not, I tell myself. Hope often comes in the darkest hour.

Perhaps it is as it must be. Perhaps we are exactly where we need to be, in order for real transformation to take place. In psychological theory, a change rarely occurs unless there is a crisis. When all is well and things are going our way, we see little reason to change. But then there is a crisis and we have the opportunity to change. *Opportunity* is the key word here, because we certainly don't have to change. We can do all in our power to get things to go back to the way they used to be. We can deny the crisis. We can cover it up, conceal it, like painting over a water stain without finding out where the water came from in the first place. We can try to manipulate the facts so we don't have to see our part in it. We can point a finger and blame others. We can engage in avoidance behaviors by distracting ourselves with all kinds of things—substances, technology, shopping, cleaning, working out, judging others . . . really, with any compulsive behavior. We can get others to bail us out, promising that we will change our ways and repay them the generosity of their loan. And all of that might work for a while. It may even work well enough and long enough that we are deluded into thinking the problem has been fixed.

But no, a crisis will happen again. It may be the same crisis with a different presentation, or it may be a totally new crisis. But be assured, unless there has been true repentance, transformation, and healing, the problem will show up again. And when that happens, we will have another opportunity to look the demon in the face. Maybe this time we can bear to really look at it—to look at what it is doing, not only to ourselves, but to others around us as well. Then we can begin the very real process of change. This usually involves grieving because we have to change our ways, something I, for one, am not always fond of doing. It involves forgiving others, and ourselves, which actually means more than feeling remorseful. It means truly repenting and doing things differently. It always involves the hard work of staying the course and being accountable.

When we allow ourselves to take this journey of change, to truly move through it, there will be a new period of things going well, of feeling good and blessed and comfortable. If we did our work, our spiritual and psychological work, the next time a crisis comes our way, we will have been formed in such a way that we trust the process of change and move through the new crisis more gracefully and quickly. Hopefully, we will have learned that we can trust in a Reality that is bigger than we are, something that may at first not have made any sense but which, with time, begins to take on meaning and purpose. When we are transformed, we realize that we exist in relationship to God, each other, and ourselves. We will know that there is true freedom in being in an intimate relationship to the Holy Other.

At some point in our lives, our souls will know winter. When it comes to us, how will we live? What will we learn?

DIGGING DEEPER

1. Perhaps there is a crisis in your life that you are pretending isn't happening. This might have something to do with relationships, health, money, job, children, or anything else of importance in your life. Summon the courage and write about it. Also try lifting it up in prayer.

2. How do you distinguish between remorse and repentance? Can you think of a time that you have been remorseful (feeling bad or guilty) but not truly repentant (ready and willing to make a change)? What is keeping you from changing your ways?

3. It is a law of physics that systems seek homeostasis. Systems do not like change. And yet, change is necessary. Can you name one aspect of your life that keeps presenting itself to you in need of change? How could a community help you make that change?

4. Is there a change happening in your family, community, or a beloved institution that is feeling like a death to you? Name that. Write about it. Talk about it.

II.

HOLY GROUND:

WORSHIP THAT TRANSFORMS, ENCOUNTERS THAT TRANSFORM

I celebrate the simple joys, the everyday joys, the ones that slip past us in only a holy flicker . . . In every life there are these small spaces of grace, the tiny reminders that life not only goes on, but goes well.

—a quote from Bishop Steven Charleston's Facebook page

Behold, I am making all things new. . . . I Write this down, for these words are trustworthy and true.

—Revelation 21:5 ESV

While all of life is sacred and holy, there are those times when the veil between heaven and earth thins. We might feel invited, metaphorically, to cross a bridge into unknown territory, sensing the potential that, on the other side, our perception will be forever changed. Or we might feel porous, more vulnerable, as if something could enter us and change our very essence. During these times, we become acutely aware of the sanctity of life and of how precious this gift of life really is. We seem to be more able to attend to the present moment, and our senses are often aroused. We may see colors more sharply, we may notice things about people that we hadn't noticed before, our ears may be more open to beautiful sounds and more aware of disturbing sounds. Our hearts may open to new feelings and thoughts, and our bodies may feel more sensitive. Skin can tingle during these thin times. Our sense of priorities can seem very clear.

Good worship is designed to create Holy Ground. It is designed to heighten our senses, open our minds and hearts, and focus our thoughts on the God of Creation. We are to be reminded of the infinite paradoxes of life during worship. We are to be strengthened to cross the bridge back into the world in which we live and to do the work we feel personally called to do. In this way we participate in the Kingdom of God in the here and now. We worship with other people to remind us that we are on this journey together. Sometimes, while worshipping, we have a holy experience. The most inspiring worship is transformative.

However, corporate worship is certainly not the only time we stand on Holy Ground. There are many things in life that remind us of the sacred. For me, the arts often evoke the Holy in life. It can be a perfect phrase of music or the sound of an instrument playing in a way that enters my skin. It can be the beauty of dancers' movements, an image in a work of art, or the depiction of a character in a play that may move me from the tedium of my daily life to an inspired, creative new mindset. I often feel changed after an encounter with the arts. Alive. Encouraged. Creative. Open. Awake.

The Celtic Christians believe that there are two books of Holy Scripture. The written word—the Bible—and the created word—the world of Nature. They believe that one without the other is incomplete. We stand on holy ground when we are experiencing God in the natural order. Many people have had an experience of the holiness of creation in the mountains, at the beach, in their garden, or perhaps just walking down the street and noticing some flowers for the first time. Something as commonplace as a brilliant full moon on a clear night, a falling leaf, sunlight on the mountainside, or standing with our feet in the water at the ocean's edge can remind us of the magnificence of creation.

Sometimes we notice holy ground when we have a profound moment in an encounter with another person. As a therapist and spiritual director, I imagine that I have had more than my fair share of these in life. That is one of the perks of the job. Yet, these precious moments are certainly not confined to an office. Ordinary conversations with friends and strangers can take on the feeling of holy ground. It is a graced moment, indeed, when we experience our connectedness as human beings. When our hearts are opened to another person, friend, or stranger, and our exchange is blessed with compassion and empathy, we have been on holy ground.

This section of the book is divided into two parts: The first part is Holy Ground: Worship. The second part is Holy Ground: Everyday Encounters. I have been transformed through many of my experiences standing on holy ground. But I confess it is easy to shield myself from them. It is easy to reject the holy invitation to see something anew. We must be willing to allow those times to change us. We must have eyes to see and ears to hear, and a heart able to allow for something new and different to happen. When we can trust ourselves to this process, the Holy One can do marvelous things.

PART ONE

HOLY GROUND:
WORSHIP THAT TRANSFORMS

Do you have eyes, but fail to see? And ears, but fail to hear?
Don't you remember?

—Mark 8:18 ISV

Laps For Jesus

Interestingly, Jesus put a child in the center of his disciples, "in the midst of them," in order to help them pay attention . . . The child was a last ditch-effort by God to help the disciples pay attention to the odd nature of God's kingdom. Few acts of Jesus are more radical, countercultural, than his blessing of children.
—Stanley Hauerwas[13]

Children are energetic, sometimes more than others, and last Sunday in church was no exception. They have a way of worshiping that reminds us of what it means to be joyful, indeed to make a joyful noise. After communion, one preschooler escaped his parent's grip, left the rail, took off and dashed around the perimeter of the seats. My pew-mate, a talented professional musician and an amateur comedian, leaned close to me and whispered, "Laps for Jesus."

There are also "Dances for Jesus." Another Sunday, while we sang "Lead On O King Eternal," two little girls joined hands and danced around each other in the aisle of the balcony. They were smiling and skipping and moving beautifully to the music, having a great time. How about "Art for Jesus"? A little boy who came in from children's chapel had made a cross, filled it with pictures of things for which he was thankful—a baseball glove, a puppy, a smiling stick figure, and what looked like a bowl of spaghetti. He clutched it in his fist with a death grip, showed it to his mother, and then to me, but there was no way he was letting go of that cross.

"Questions for Jesus" could be another category. As I watched the children moving and worshiping in their kinetic ways, I recalled a four-year-old at the communion rail with me, probably fifteen years earlier. "What's in the glass? Is it beer?" he shouted loudly as his father, the priest, brought the chalice to my lips. My own daughter, as a middle-school student, asked, " Mama, what's the difference between magic and mystery?" And a visiting child from a nearby community asked me, "Why are all the men dressed up like women?"

Another favorite of mine is "Food for Jesus." I remember sitting in church next to a family with preschool-age twin girls. After communion, the mother took out a Tupperware container filled with Cheerios. The two eagerly dug into their snack and offered me a few of those oat circles, stuck to their saliva-coated fingers. "The Body of Christ," the little girl mumbled to me as she held the tiny circle up to my mouth. How could I resist? Watching a new mom nurse her baby as we sang "Let Us Break Bread Together" brought me to tears one Sunday, many years ago.

During his sermon one Sunday, a priest friend of mine shared his memory of lying on his back in the pews at his Catholic church on Long Island, looking at the art painted on the ceiling of the sanctuary. Angels and puffy clouds, cherubim and seraphim floating in the sky. This depiction touched him, he said, and he thought about heaven in that way for a long time.

We may not be able to describe scientifically what happens to children who attend church Sunday after Sunday, but I believe something deeply and profoundly formational happens. When children hear the songs week after week, listen to the prayers and chants, kneel at the rail, look at the art, taste the bread and the wine, rock in their parent's or a grandparent's arms, they are being formed, nourished, and loved in ways we cannot even imagine. They are learning the sights, sounds, and smells of culture and community. For all the problems with the institutional church, for all the disagreements I can have with the theology and praxis of the church, our secular culture still has no substitute for this. If we want our children to carry with them the beauty and joy of worship, the nurture and support of community, the mystery of God in Christ, then we must take them, week after week, to the place where that can happen. We must bring them to worship with us. Even when we wonder if it's worth the effort to get out of the house and go. Even when we spend most of the service keeping them occupied with coloring books and snacks. Even when we get embarrassed by their playful antics and loud comments. As difficult as it can be sometimes, we must take them with us and keep ourselves open to what they have to teach us. Pay close attention to what they do and say. It just might change your life.

Digging Deeper

1. What have you learned from being with or watching a child during worship?

2. Jesus said we must become like children. What do you think he meant?

3. What is your comfort level with children in worship? How do you react when a child is misbehaving? Eating? Fidgeting?

4. Children are so comfortable asking questions about God. Imagine you are a little child and make a list of your questions. Perhaps you could be brave enough to ask them in a group or with a friend. If not, certainly hold them up in prayer.

Love with Wild Abandon

The soul is healed by being with children.
—Fyodor Dostoevsky[14]

The children come back into the sanctuary for communion. They have been at Sunday school for the "Gospel Experience," a time when they hear and read the Gospel, and then do a small art project to enhance their learning. When they rejoin the congregation, they process (it's more like a parade) down the center aisle, one or two of them proudly carrying a kid-size wooden cross and the rest straggling behind, holding their craft project of the day, looking for the familiar face of mom or dad, sometimes of a grandmother or grandfather. Parents wave at them to say, "Here I am, honey." Sometimes a parent steps from the pew and whispers the child's name, and some parents come to the front of the church so they can be easily seen for the few children who are still a bit anxious after having left mommy or daddy. It's all done quietly with decorum, the organ usually humming some simple, unrecognizable tune in the background. The rest of us stand, watch, and smile as the little ones, very unselfconsciously, find their way back to their families.

And then there's the one, there's usually one, who's searching the crowd for the face that will mean "I'm home," and when he finds it he yells with total abandon, "MAMA!" and breaks into a run and leaps into her arms. It always catches the rest of us up into a subdued laugh, a few "aahs," and some big smiles. This past Sunday there was "the one" and then later after communion, there was another. Returning with her parents from the rail, the girl spotted a familiar face up in the balcony, and from across the church shouted, "I see you, MeeMa," and jumped up and down and waved.

Hooray for the kids who love and cherish with that kind of abandon. I feel it, that kind of wild happiness, when I see someone I love, someone I haven't seen in a while, especially one I am waiting for. When my daughter comes home, my whole body is awaiting the sound of her car in the driveway. I am usually keeping watch, and after I shout "Maria's home," I rush outside for the first of many hugs. It's usually a longer hug, and it is always sweet. I even feel that way with friends I've been missing and am happily anticipating seeing. I have a friend in Canada whom I don't see often, but I love to call her. If her husband answers the phone, his greeting always makes me smile and even giggle, because he always says, "AMY," as if my call has made his day.

When we love each other like this, when we call each other's names and welcome each other with wild abandon, we are, I believe, replicating the kingdom of God. Can you imagine God seeing you from a distance and calling out your name with utter joy, perhaps even waving at you to let you know you're in the right place? I believe that happens. Now, flip the coin for a moment. Do you call out God's name, "O HOLY ONE," with abandon when you get a glimpse of the Divine? When you shut your eyes to pray, or stop to watch a sunset, or eat something scrumptious, or are surprised by some amazing grace in your life, do you call out, "BLESSED GOD"? Do you love God with enough wild abandon that when you are in creation, hearing the whoosh as a dolphin surfaces or seeing a rabbit's nose twitch or silently watching your child sleep, you can say, either wordlessly or aloud, "Surely you, God, are in this place."

Hooray for the children, who remind us of the exuberance of God's love. May we never "shush" them, may we emulate the way they love with wild abandon.

DIGGING DEEPER

1. In what ways are you most passionate about your faith? What, if any, messages have you gotten in life that may have dampened your exuberance? Where? From whom?

2. What would it look like if you were to greet God with wild abandon?

3. Picture yourself in a Bible story that evokes a wild sense of abandon. Give yourself time to visualize yourself as a character in it. I like to imagine myself as the woman who poured expensive oil all over Jesus. That kind of loving with wild abandon speaks to me. What speaks to you? This is a wonderful activity to do with a group.

4. Think about an area of your life where you could practice being more passionate, more spontaneous, more free. It could be as simple as singing in the shower or dancing in the kitchen. Perhaps you would like to be freer with your expressions of love with those close to you. Whatever the situation, make a commitment to pick just one way to love with more abandon.

Prepare My Heart

When we were children, we used to think that when we were grown-up we would no longer be vulnerable. But to grow up is to accept vulnerability. To be alive is to be vulnerable.
—Madeline L'Engle[15]

When I was a child, I spoke and thought and reasoned as a child does. But when I grew up, I put away childish things.
—1 Corinthians 13:11 NLT

True and true. That is the nature of paradox. The opposite of a truth is another equal truth. And that is the nature of worship.

Most Sundays I try to get to worship early enough to sit in silence and enter into prayer. Often the words "prepare my heart" come to my attention as I take my first few quiet but deep breaths. This past Sunday as I thought "Prepare my heart, O God," my mind wandered off to a household project I've got going on right now.

My husband and I are painting our master bedroom and hiring a professional to do a special finish on one of the walls. The walls are being prepared. We are dusting, washing, spackling, and sanding. We may put on a primer coat because we are making a significant color change. All of this is being done in order for the new paint to *take* properly. To *stick*. Good painters will tell you that the hardest work is the preparation of the walls. After that, putting up color is the easy part.

Prepare my heart. What do I need to wash away before worship can *take*? What holes need to be filled, what rough edges need to be sanded away so that my heart can worship, can open to the Holy

Other and truly be in relationship with the Mystery. What needs to happen for the sacrament that we call the Holy Eucharist to *stick*?

I have participated in many rituals in my life. Some of them have been within the bounds of organized religion: baptisms and brises, confirmations and bar mitzvahs, weddings and funerals. Many of them have been outside this realm: universal dances for peace, African rituals to remember the dead, sweat lodges, art circles, writer's circles, and certain therapy sessions. Properly designed and enacted, rituals create an altered state, a state in which the ego takes a back seat and its defenses are lowered, our receptivity and creativity are heightened, and we are open to the Mystery, open to things we cannot and do not understand but experience nonetheless. When a ritual *sticks*, when it *takes*, we are changed and we know it. We haven't just "gone to church" another Sunday; we have been changed. Sometimes we don't have the words to explain what we are feeling. We might have a felt sense, an inner knowing that things will be different going forward. We may not want to talk about it at all because it might feel too private or sacred, but we know we've been changed.

The children we see at church are often vulnerable. They are so present, so spontaneous. So in the moment. We adults have trained ourselves out of this, unless we worship in the charismatic tradition. We don't cry out when we see our loved ones. We don't jump up and down in joy when we leave the altar. We don't clap. Instead we smile at each other politely, give sideways hugs or handshakes when passing the peace, lower our eyes at the communion rail, and pray in the accepted tradition. There is so much decorum. We have found a way to tame the childhood chaos and to agree on how we will join in worshiping the Holy One. It is not bad. This is not a judgment. It is just a comment on how hard we have made it for worship to *stick*. If we have to keep our egos and intellects front and center, if we have to contain our emotions, our sense of joy and sorrow, we have made it more difficult for the Holy Other to take hold.

Once at Kanuga Camp and Conference Center in the mountains of North Carolina, I participated with Malidoma Somé, an African elder, in a ritual that took all day. It began early in the morning when he asked us to pay attention, as we walked around the campus, to things we might want to place on the altar. What in nature called to us that day and why? Malidoma Somé asked us to be particularly aware of our loved ones who had died and to see if there was a way that we could remember them through the natural world. As the day went on, the altar began to take on an energy all its own as participants prayerfully placed special remembrances there. At sunset the large conference room was prepared with incense and prayer. The musicians began drumming and we joined by making percussive music with rattles and other noisemakers. We were tuning into our heartbeat.

The evening continued as Malidoma and the other leaders asked participants to come up to the altar and open their hearts to the wisdom of the deceased. People danced, wept, slept, hugged, meditated, and made music. Four hours later, we all limped to our beds, exhausted. I dreamt deeply that evening of my paternal grandmother as she spoke words that have been healing to me. It felt like I heard words from beyond the grave. The ritual did what rituals are supposed to do. Hours after it began, my heart was prepared to listen.

When we come to worship on any given day, it is hard to make enough space for our hearts to be truly prepared. How is it possible to make the transition from work or home to worshipping? Somehow, we must allow ourselves to become vulnerable. As Madeline L'Engle's statement suggests, it is only in being vulnerable that we are truly alive. Without vulnerability, worship is dead. Without vulnerability, the Spirit has no real power. Without vulnerability, we are dead.

While we can no longer be children, we must find ways to come to Jesus with open hearts. Beginners' hearts. Hearts that are breaking. Hearts that are overflowing. Then, and only then, can true worship stick. Prepare our hearts, O God.

DIGGING DEEPER

∞

1. How do you prepare yourself for worship?

2. These are words from a chant by Jason Shulman that I was taught by a friend:

   > Unlock my heart O God
   > Unlock my mind
   > Unlock my spirit, too
   > I give it all to you

   Consider memorizing these words and repeat them over and over again at the beginning of worship. You can try alternating lines with an inhalation and an exhalation.

3. What have been the most meaningful rituals in your life? What made them so? If you are in a group, consider sharing these experiences with each other.

4. What is the difference between the times you leave worship feeling changed and those times when you leave feeling empty and dry?

5. How would you explain your experience of being vulnerable?

The Oneness of Time

*What appears to be the past and the future is in fact the same home,
the same call, and the same God, for whom "a thousand years are like a
single day" (Psalm 90:4 GW) and a single day like a thousand years.*

*Some would call this homing device their soul, and some would call it
the indwelling Holy Spirit, and some might call it nostalgia or dreamtime.
All I know is that it will not be ignored. It calls us both backward and
forward, to our foundation and our future, at the same time. It also feels
like grace from within us and at the same time beyond us. The soul lives
in such eternally deep time.*

—Richard Rohr[16]

I am acutely aware recently of what seems like another paradox, the
reality of which has turned my life upside down. I often find myself,
in the present moment, anticipating a future moment. In the present
moment, as I pay attention to it, the feeling that is real, and sometimes intensely, is an anticipation of what is to be a future experience.

On a Monday just a few short weeks ago, I was scheduled
for a session with my massage therapist. Throughout the day, as
I was "checking in" with myself, I realized that my whole body
was anticipating the massage. I could almost feel the warm hands
on my neck and back, and just breathing in the memory of past
massages seemed to calm me. I still felt very present to my daily
routine, but I was definitely anticipating an event that was yet to
come later that day because of an experience I had had in the past.

Again, this time in church on a Sunday, I found myself anticipating communion. During the singing of the anthem, as I closed

my eyes to listen more closely, I found myself almost tasting the bread and the wine on my tongue. I could hear the words, "The Blood of Christ, shed for you." In the present moment, listening as closely as I could to the choir, I was sensing the future moment of sipping the Eucharistic cup, a drink I had had innumerable times before.

And so I have been thinking of the kinds of things I actively anticipate. I anticipate wonderful meals, especially if I am the one preparing them. Perhaps I have tasted the food during preparation, checking on the appropriate amount of spice, so I already know how wonderful it will be when it is time to sit down to the meal. I may have made this recipe before, and I remember how fabulous it was. I anticipate luxuriating in the company of certain friends, and I anticipate spending time with family. I anticipate the sound of my husband's car in the driveway when he comes home from a business trip. Sometimes I anticipate my yoga practice, knowing how good it will feel to open my body and breathe into tight and stuck places. I anticipate the smell and sound of the ocean when I cross the bridge to Sullivan's Island. I could go on for a long time.

I find myself wondering about all the books I've read on being present. What would the gurus of being in the present moment say to me? Eckhart Tolle in *The Power of Now* and *A New Earth*, Thich Nhat Hanh in *Being Peace*, Anthony de Mello in *Awareness*? I've read them all and have benefited from learning how to stay present, only in this very moment. Yet, here I am, in the present moment, anticipating the future by remembering the past. I know I live in a world where time is linear, but in those moments when linear time falls away, I know that there is no beginning and no ending. I am encircled in time, remembering the past, being in the present, and anticipating the future all at once. It makes perfect sense to me. I can have a "foretaste of the feast to come" because I've had a feast in the past. I can "remember his death, proclaim his resurrection, and await his coming in glory," as Episcopalians say in Eucharistic Prayer II, all in the same moment. Past, present, and future as one.

If we can perceive time in this way, we have the potential to see time as abundant, a perception that would challenge most of us. In America, we perceive time as scarce. "There's never enough time in a day. If I just had enough time. The only thing I need is more time." Such comments are common in our culture. The Benedictine Rule counters this, teaching basic concepts about time. First, there is enough time each day for the things that are important—study, worship, community, and work. Paradoxically, by allotting space in the day for these four priorities, time becomes more available. The Rule of Life, which at the very least gives a rhythm to each day, seems to make time more circular, as if there is no beginning and there is no ending. Following the Benedictine Way, we can transcend linear time. As Benedictine Sister Joan Chittister says, "We have all the time there is."

It is impossible to relinquish entirely our view of time as linear and limited. We can, however, practice perceiving time as abundant. What if we are really living in Eternity right now? Would it not be transformational to say every day, "There is enough time for what is important"? Or try this one: "There is a time for everything under heaven." Perhaps as we enter a church season like Advent or Lent, a season of waiting, preparation, and anticipation, we can remember that there is enough time because there's always been enough time, and there always will be enough time. That's the way the Creator made it.

DIGGING DEEPER

∞

1. If you were trying to convey the concept of time to an alien, how would you explain it?
2. Everyone has a different method of dealing with time and time restrictions. What is yours?
3. What does the phrase "We have all the time in the world" mean to you?
4. Have you ever experienced yourself outside of space and time? Try to capture that experience in words or pictures.
5. Jesus talks about being outside of space and time:

> When I saw him, I fell at his feet as though dead. But he placed his right hand on me, saying, "Do not be afraid; I am the first and the last, and the living one."
> —Revelation 1:17–18

> As you go, proclaim the good news, "The kingdom of heaven has come near." Cure the sick, raise the dead, cleanse the lepers, cast out demons. You received without payment; give without payment.
> —Matthew 10:7–9

What other verses from Scripture teach this same concept? What poems or other literature are you familiar with that illustrate this concept of time as spiraling and eternal?

Thanks Be To God

For the fruit of all creation, thanks be to God.
For his gifts to every nation, thanks be to God.
For the plowing, sowing, reaping,
Silent growth when we are sleeping,
Future seeds in earth's safekeeping, thanks be to God.

For the just reward of labor, God's will be done.
For the help we give our neighbor, God's will be done.
In our world-wide task of caring,
For the hungry and despairing,
In the harvests we are sharing, God's will be done.

For the harvests of the Spirit, thanks be to God.
For the good we all inherit, thanks be to God,
For the wonders that astound us,
For the truths that still confound us,
Most of all that love has found us, thanks be to God.

—Hymn 424
Words by F. Pratt Green[17]

We all have our favorite hymns. As a child I loved "A Mighty Fortress Is Our God." I loved the melody because it felt strong to me, and, being a German Lutheran at the time, strong was important. I thought it was cool that Martin Luther, the man whose life I had to study in my three years of confirmation class, wrote hymns, and he wrote that one. Somehow Luther's confidence about God was contagious and I felt connected to that confidence when I sang that song. I knew it from memory by the time I was in my teens.

As a teenager I must have needed to know that a strong, all-pow-
erful God would save me from any mortal ills. I always sang it
with gusto.

Today one of my favorite hymns is "Thanks Be To God." The
melody is gentle and rolling, but it does build nicely, giving the
singer a chance to put some oomph into the song. I like the combi-
nation of the gentleness and the strength of the melody, but I think
it is the words that really speak to me.

In verse one, we start out globally. We are told that creation
everywhere bears fruit, and that God blesses every nation and
all people. How do you imagine that happening? And then we
are reminded that we are not in charge of creation, that there is
"Silent growth when we are sleeping / Future needs in earth's safekeeping." God is at work when we are sleeping, taking care of
the future before we even ask. This reminds me that a few years
ago researchers proved what mothers around the world had been
saying since the beginning of time. Children grow in their sleep.
"Nonsense," women were told when they exclaimed this at a doctor's visit. "You just didn't notice the small amounts of growth
until they accumulated and then at that moment you noticed."
Finally, the research proved (as if mothers everywhere had needed
the proof) that children indeed grow in their sleep, sometimes
overnight. Ahh . . . the mystery of creation.

In verse two, F. Pratt Green reminds us that it is God's will
that people be given a just reward for their labor, and that we love
our neighbor, feed the poor, and share our harvests. The eight
United Nations' Millennium Development Goals (the elimination
of poverty, universal education, gender equality, child health care,
maternal health care, combat HIV/AIDS, environmental sustain-
ability, and global partnerships) give us a very concrete way of following the imperative of this verse. It is God's will that people
everywhere be fed, educated, and kept safe and healthy. In the
wake of hurricanes, tsunamis, starvation, and terrorist attacks, this

verse might remind us to make a special donation to a charity of our choice. It might encourage us to work at a soup kitchen, to buy food for a family that needs it, to volunteer at a school as a mentor or helper, or to volunteer for a mission trip.

My favorite verse is the last. We *inherit* good, all of us. We are part of the human story that has been unfolding since the beginning of time. Our short time on earth is just another moment in this unfolding, and we have inherited all of the accomplishments, knowledge, and wisdom of those who have gone before us. It is appropriate to be astounded and confounded, because God's creation is too wonderful to comprehend. If we but take the time to look and watch, we will be speechless and a bit puzzled. We cannot possibly tame the Holy Mystery. Thanks be to God.

It is easy to stand up in church on Sunday mornings and sing the hymns, forgetting that language is a powerful former and transformer. We come to believe what we say and sing, internalizing the message and the image without necessarily being consciously aware of it. Try picking out a favorite hymn. Pick out one that evokes a profound yearning in you, one that calls you to a deeper connection with the Holy. So many of them are beautiful poetry, meant to help us sing out our faith and praise God. Many of them are complicated theological comments, and we may not always agree with the theology they express. Some may speak to us more at a particular time in our life or during a particular season. Just pick one. Use it as a meditation for your week. Sing it during a walk or around the dinner table. Sing it out in the shower or while doing the yard work. Teach it to your children. Hum it while making dinner or getting dressed. Let the tune and the poetry become a part of you for a while. God will speak to you in a new way.

DIGGING DEEPER

1. What are some of your favorite hymns? What is it about one of those hymns that make it a favorite? Write the words of the hymn in a journal. Consider memorizing them.

2. Sometimes a hymn will speak to us during a particular situation in our lives or at the time of a specific hardship. You may want to make note of these in a journal and share them with a friend or a group.

3. Sometimes there are hymns that grate on our nerves or bother us. What are those hymns for you? Notice why you don't like them. Language? Music? Unhappy associations?

4. If you are in a small group, it would be great fun to have a "Favorite Hymn Sing" for one of your meetings. Spend the time sharing favorites, talking about the "why" of each hymn, and just enjoy singing along. If there is a pianist available, supplying accompaniment would be an added bonus.

The Cathedral Concert

"Our own words" are inadequate even to express the meaning of other words; how much more inadequate, when it is a matter of rendering meanings which have their original expression in terms of music.
—Aldous Huxley[18]

I was sitting in Trinity Cathedral, Columbia, South Carolina, but it could have been St. Paul's in London, Notre Dame in Paris, or the Basilica in Assisi. In each of these places, my experience has been similar. I feel cradled in a safe place, a familiar place. I know the plaster walls, some cracked and stained, the large columns, floor to ceiling, holding up the roof, tile floors chipped, worn, and echoing. Light pours through the stained glass, sweeping rivers of color across the ceiling and walls. The high altar is covered in starched white linens, brass vases of perfectly arranged flowers flanked by tall candles on either end. For just the right medieval touch, a resident bat is flying above the nave, fluttering beyond the reach of ushers and priests.

The orchestra began its warm-up, every musician playing a few notes or phrases that needed a last-minute review or touch-up. I love that sound, one phrase, one melody on top of another, none matching, each musician intensely focused on a particular section of a piece. The complexity of that sound, the sheer confusion and fullness of it heightens my senses, until suddenly it all stops and there is total silence. The conductor and soloist walk in, the applause dies down, and the congregation releases a collective breath of anticipation.

The concert began with an organ concerto. Poulenc. It rolled around in my ears like a sip of fine wine rolls around the mouth. I noticed different things at different times: a fine viola section, the human-like voice of the cello, the organ, paradoxically light and cascading one minute, layered and expansive the next. The timpani, offering an undercurrent, made a vibration that went straight to my core. The tension. The release. The perfection. I wondered, as I often do when listening to the music of the masters, about the brilliance and giftedness of the composer. What kind of hearts and minds write music like this? How do they imagine all the parts in their heads and in their ears? Surely, I always imagine, they have a direct line of some kind to the Divine. And then my heart fills with love and thanksgiving for the musicians. The sheer number of hours of practice, training, devotion, and coordination needed to accomplish this moves me. I know that somehow, through the music, they remember what is important in the world and they remind the rest of us of this. They say with the music that which we cannot say with words. I am reminded of a plaque in my home that reads, "For heights and depths no words can reach, music is the soul's own speech."

During the break as the organ was moved off center and risers were set up for the choristers, new musicians joined the orchestra. Durufle's *Requiem* was the next selection. I noticed the boys and girls' choir in the left balcony. The young people buzzed with smiles and excitement, and I was hoping they were somehow going to be a part of the music. Again the silence, and again the applause as we settled in to receive the next gift. By the time the Kyrie was over, I was utterly transported. Surely this was the music of heaven. Is it possible that this is mostly a volunteer choir? Just regular people like me, joining their voices with the grace of God to make music that soars, lifts, humbles, and inspires? By this time, I was so full I was weeping.

The moment continued in this beautiful vein, and I kept breathing and receiving and allowing myself to go wherever the music took me. The children soon sang. "Pie Jesu, sweet Jesus." Sweet Jesus, indeed, must have been right there in the cathedral. Their sound was compelling, clear, one voice, one breath, coming from on high. But what struck me the most was the relationship these children seemed to have with the choir director. They seemed locked to each other, joined by eyes and lips and hearts and breath.

The requiem ended peacefully. A full silence. A perfect silence. May it be so for each of us at the end, I thought. Wherever that is. Wherever I am. Columbia? London? Paris? Assisi? Amen.

DIGGING DEEPER

∞

1. When was the last time you were moved to tears by music, dance, poetry, or art?
2. In what ways could you support the arts in your community or churches?
3. How is performing or creating art like worship?
4. How is witnessing or observing art like worship?
5. If you were in charge of worship, what kind of service would you create? What would it look like? Sound like? Feel like? What would you want people to experience?

PART TWO

HOLY GROUND:

ENCOUNTERS THAT TRANSFORM

Where is the door to God?
In the sound of a barking dog,
In the ring of a hammer,
In a drop of rain,
In the face of
Everyone
I see.

—Hafiz[19]

Holding Sacred Space

Your soul and my soul
Once sat together in the Beloved's womb
Playing footsie.
Your heart and my heart
Are very, very old
Friends.
—Hafiz[20]

It was cold yesterday morning, and I pulled my hood up as I walked along the streets in my neighborhood. I focused on the silhouettes of the budding dogwoods against the dawn sky, the newly opened azaleas, the daffodils, hyacinths, and tulips. Spring in Columbia is beautiful. I was breathing it in. It was a prayer, this gratitude for God's created world. I enjoy paying attention to the created order in the early morning hours. Sometimes I get answers to questions or concerns just by walking and breathing and paying attention. Mostly, though, I just like to rest in the lap of God's creation.

Looking ahead, I could see her in the distance walking toward me. I know her gait and her shape, and I crossed the street to say good morning to my friend. We hadn't planned on meeting. I know sometimes I don't want to be interrupted when I am walking/praying. But she waved and said hello, turned off her headphones, and we started walking side by side. We've met like this before, and our conversations always seem to be a special time of sharing. Today was no different.

The last time we walked I had been sharing some about a friendship, some old wounds I had incurred, and the state of their healing. Like a patient with an open sore, I was reporting the condition of things. "It's better, I think. Oozing less, scabbing up pretty nicely. It doesn't hurt so much anymore, unless I accidentally bump it and then, ouch, I sure know it's not completely healed. But it's better, and I am grateful. Most important, I know it will heal. I believe that. And please, don't let me whine," I implored. I hate whining. She assured me that there is a difference between sharing and whining.

Today she was sharing. I am accustomed to listening. I do it for a living. It is a gift, and it brings me joy. I was aware immediately that I was honored by her trust in me, and our developing trust in each other. We had both shared stories that leave us very vulnerable, stories that hint at the essence of who and what we are. At the end of the walk, we hugged and she said, "This is sacred space. Let's hold our talks in our hearts."

As I left her on the corner and headed home, I thought, "This is also prayer, another kind of prayer. Creating sacred space with another, holding another's heart in our hearts, is prayer." I knew I had been changed by this encounter.

This is what God must do. Our hearts are held in the heart of the Holy One. In that Heart of Hearts, all the hearts of the world live together. I can even imagine holding the heart of God in my heart, as I did this morning on an early walk with a friend. What a precious and sacred way of praying.

DIGGING DEEPER

1. Recall a time when an encounter with a friend felt holy. What made it that way? Take the time to journal about that experience. Share it with your friend.

2. With whom are you most likely to allow yourself to be vulnerable? How do you allow others to "hold your heart"?

3. How do you give your heart into God's keeping? What does that feel like and look like to you?

4. Imagine that you are holding God's heart. What image comes to mind as you imagine this? Could you draw or paint it?

A Moment of Truth

This is the first, the wildest
and the wisest thing I know:
that the soul exists and is built entirely out of attentiveness.
—Mary Oliver[21]

Banking online has changed my life. I was the most skeptical and paranoid newcomer to this technology, but now I regard it as a miracle. I love the convenience of not having to wait for my monthly statement to come in the mail and being able to reconcile my checkbook at any time of night or day. I find it amazing that I am able to transfer money with the click of a button. I can send my daughter money from my home office simply by pointing and clicking. Voilà. Presto. Money flies between accounts. And the bill paying? Wow, is that mighty slick. No check writing, no stamps, no envelopes. Because of it, I almost never go into a bank building.

But last week I needed to close an account and ask a real person some questions, so I entered the bank and talked to a young man, probably in his mid-twenties. After helping me with my business, I asked if he could give me an estimate on refinancing my mortgage. Interest rates were dropping again, and I thought it wouldn't hurt to ask. He started talking to me about interest rates and credit cards. I don't know how it happened or where the segue was, but rather quickly he began sharing his fears and concerns about *his* finances. I was in the conversation before I had a chance to think.

Let me back up a moment. My husband used to tell me that I had an invisible sign saying "Talk to Me" tattooed on my forehead.

I could be standing in grocery lines and someone in front of me or behind me would start telling me about their ailing mother or their out-of-control teenager. Total strangers. Once I was opening the door to my car in the mall parking lot and the person at the next car started telling me about her husband at home with Parkinson's and how this was her first day out in over a month. I stood there for twenty minutes just listening and reassuring. I was late picking up my child because I didn't know how to end the conversation. I have worked very hard to have more control over this invisible tattoo on my forehead. For example, I've learned to avert my eyes, which seem to be the invitation. I've learned to pull my energy in, to be more self-contained and less "out there." I've learned to be more selective in my listening and less welcoming with my gaze. It's self-preservation. I do this for a living. I don't need to be doing it at the grocery store.

Back to the bank. So here I am, listening to this young man. He has too much credit card debt. He bought a new car. It will take him two years to get out of debt, if he can stop spending. Ah, there's the rub. He smirks as he admits he has trouble not overspending. Maybe a move will help, a higher-paying job. This bank doesn't pay as well as he'd like. I say an encouraging few words like, "Two years is nothing in the big picture. Stick with it, pay off your debt. You'll be proud of yourself, you'll get some professional momentum going, and the time will pass quickly." He continues about all the options and about how his parents would kill him if they knew how much debt he had. He keeps talking, and then, before I can stop myself, I blurt out this question: *Do you believe what the culture has taught you?*

"What?" He looks me straight in the eyes, startled.

I repeat. "Do you believe what your culture has taught you?"

"You mean about money?" he quizzes me.

"Yeah. But it's about life, too," I say. "Do you believe that money will make you happy?"

No answer. Wrinkles in the forehead. A sigh.

"It won't. It will buy you choices, and that is one kind of freedom. But it won't buy you happiness or real freedom," I offer tentatively. He is quiet, pensive.

"I am so sorry," I continue. "My daughter is in her twenties. I know you've all been assaulted with this message. She has, too. It makes me sad, and I feel responsible for my part in this. I tried to fight it, you know, parenting her, but I'm not sure I succeeded."

Now I'm rambling and he's listening, nodding. And the conversation moves easily back and forth between us. I look at my watch and get up quickly. I have to be at the office in just a few minutes.

"Thanks for the encouragement," he says as he walks me to the front door. "I needed that."

"Good to meet you," I say.

Whatever just happened, I am aware as I back out of the parking spot that it was precious. We entered each other's world, two people unlikely to be connected by much. We touched each other for just a moment. We were authentic together, for just a moment. We told each other a truth of ours, for just a moment. And we held sacred space, for just a moment. Perhaps I'll go back into the real bank building again before too much time passes.

DIGGING DEEPER

1. When were you last surprised by God? If you are participating in a group discussion, you may want to talk about when you were last surprised in the group.

2. How might you find holy ground in everyday encounters?

3. There are many reasons we engage or don't engage with others. When are you most likely to allow yourself to engage with a stranger?

4. People often credit their intuition for telling them when it is safe to engage with a stranger. How do you use your intuition in situations with strangers?

Together on Holy Ground

What matters
is that, when I saw them,
I saw them
As through the veil, secretly, joyfully, clearly.
—Mary Oliver[22]

"There sure is a lot of estrogen floating around in this room," a male staff person said to me as he helped me move a table to get ready for a women's retreat.

I laughed.

"Yeah, you better be careful. You never know what will happen when a group of women gets together for a weekend."

He nodded and raised an eyebrow, as if the mystery of women truly left him puzzled.

When he left the room I stopped a moment just to soak it all in. Some women, standing in the corner, were laughing, gesturing with their hands as they listened to a story or joke. Two women were "fussing" with tablecloths, candles, and flowers, making things pretty and soft for the rest of us. One woman was rubbing a friend's shoulders as they sat on a couch together. A musician was tuning her instrument and practicing a song. There *was* a lot of estrogen floating around that room. The sacred space was being prepared.

My husband reports that men's weekends have a similar feel to them, although the details are different. Cutting branches to build a sweat lodge, physical tasks undertaken to build interdependence, and the telling of nighttime dreams are things that support the building of a community of men. These activities are designed to draw our attention to the present moment, to help us notice and honor the sacred space that is being created, and to transport us to *this* place and time when all else is put aside and we come together with an intention—to expect to have a Holy experience.

For a community to hold sacred space, to come together in an intimate way, many small miracles have to happen. First, there has to be room for each person's thoughts, opinions, and feelings. When we participate in community, we have to be willing and able to hear from someone who is not like us and to be influenced by them. While doing that, we have to be simultaneously true to who we are and to let ourselves be open to the other. In community, it is always best if the members have a stated intention to open up to something bigger (the Holy Other, the Mystery) and to loosen the grip on our egos. I could stop right there. That would be miraculous enough.

If we were to hope for something even more intimate and transformative than being open and true to ourselves and others, if we could hope that something essential would happen to us, that something would break through and really matter to us as we gather in a group, then we would have to be willing to be vulnerable. All the ways that we present ourselves to others, all of the tricks we have to keep ourselves safe and sound, all the ways we are used to defining ourselves would have to be shed so that we could become closer to the true Essence of our beings. And in that space, what we often discover is that we are not much different from one another. The things that divide us—race, creed, religion, family, culture, sexual orientation and money, to name a few—pass away, and we are, all of us, on the same journey back to our ultimate Home.

I gather in a circle of women once a month. It is a time clearly marked on my calendar, and I anticipate it just as a child anticipates Christmas. In this circle, I know I am welcome, just the way I am. I know I can cry, grieve, laugh, celebrate, and anguish. I will be missed if I am absent. There are weeks when someone is laughing and someone else is crying. No one needs to be fixed because we are all accepted just the way we are. This is community. When we are together there is space for anything that needs to be. I don't play a role (therapist, spiritual director, mother, wife, friend). I just *am*. I want to be known here for who I am with all of my humanity. I want to celebrate my gifts and accept and challenge my flaws. I want to accept others in the same way.

I also facilitate several support groups for clergy. For two hours, once a month, a group of clergy meet. Over time as trust develops and sacred space is held, the role of pastor or priest can fade away and now there is a place to just be. Finally, there are no expectations, no "shoulds" and "oughts," no need to present oneself in a certain light, and nothing to fear. The members of the group gain a sense of integrity, of wholeness, of being loved and accepted for who they are with all the light and all the darkness.

This is Holy Ground—these groups where one can be fully human and fully alive, fully accepted and fully challenged. In these groups the Holy Spirit can move whatever needs to be moved to continue the work of making us more like Christ, more human, more divine. Surely God is in these places.

DIGGING DEEPER

∞

Surely God is in this place. Holy Ground.

Be silent, still, aware / For there in my own heart the Spirit is at prayer. / Listen and learn, / Open and find / Heart wisdom / Christ.

1. Above are two brief prayers that I use from time to time. Pick one of them and memorize it. Try to repeat it throughout the day. Make a note of how it is affecting you.

2. If you have ever been part of a group that has truly felt like Holy Ground, think about the following questions: How did the group create that quality of Holy Ground? What were the characteristics and qualities of the group? If you have not had this experience, think about what has prevented that from happening.

3. How does the sacred ground in groups get sabotaged? If you have had this experience, what were the dynamics in the group that allowed this to happen? If you hurt in a way that has had long-term consequences, how would you say this has affected your desire or willingness to be vulnerable and trusting in group settings?

4. Try creating a short prayer or phrase that reminds you of the Holy Ground you inhabit every day.

Evangelism

Every generation has to be converted anew, and the Gospel has to be preached in new contexts and cultures in ways that are good news to that time and people.
—Richard Rohr[23]

New technology pretty much freaks me out. It seems like I just get used to a particular phone, radio, computer, even coffee pot, and it's time for a new one. Then, I have to learn something different because it's all new and improved. The old buttons aren't there anymore. There may not even *be* buttons or prompts. Now there are touch dials, touch pads, or voice commands. For me this creates anxiety and I seem to have minimal ability to focus and "just spend extra time with it," as my techie friends always tell me. Time? Are they kidding?

When I decided to buy an Apple MacBook laptop, I knew it would be a new language and technology, but the pros seemed to outweigh the cons, so I made my purchase to the cheers of my daughter and other friends who are Mac enthusiasts. I went into the whole process with the attitude that I would be learning something new, that I would give myself plenty of grace, and that I would try not to get exasperated. Lots of deep breathing, I told myself, and no rush jobs. Nothing last minute.

I am still breathing deeply, and thanks to a visit to the Apple Store in Charleston, South Carolina, I survived. I visited the store because I was having trouble with some very basic things, like saving stuff to my flash drive, sending documents to my assistant, and getting handouts formatted correctly. When I walked in the door, a delightful and funky man greeted me.

"How can we help you today?" he said.

"I need a kindergarten teacher," I replied. I was trying really hard to look bright and enthusiastic. "I just got this laptop. I'm in the 'Technology for Dummies' class."

He pressed a button on a wire next to his ear and called for Ryan.

"Ryan, do you have some time? I have a customer that needs you."

Enter Ryan. Dark, bearded, wide brown eyes, relaxed. He was wearing an aqua-colored T-shirt printed with words that spanned the width of his chest: *"I could talk about this stuff for hours."* Perfect, I thought. It might take hours.

"How can I help you today?"

"Ryan, how patient are you?" I asked. And then, with much apology, I told him my problems as I took my Mac out of its case.

"I just don't get it," I said too many times to count. "I don't get how to set up a file in this program, and I don't get how to transfer my files from my old computer, and I don't get how to find my downloads, and I don't get how to check for updates, and I don't get . . ."—I repeated it over and over until I was almost breathless with the repetition of it.

And every time I said it, Ryan listened carefully to me, checked out my computer, showed me how to do it, and showed me again if I asked. He consulted another person for help with one of my questions that was confusing him, and came back with an answer that solved not only that problem but also another one I was having. Periodically I would say, "Do you need to help anyone else? Am I keeping you too long?" The answer was always some variation of, "Absolutely not. I can stay with you until we're done. I don't work on commission. Take your time."

He also told me about a program called "One-to-One" which gives a customer up to one hour a week of personal tutoring. I was almost shivering with excitement until he told me it's only offered at Mac stores so I couldn't get it in my hometown of Columbia. I left the Apple Store feeling many emotions. Relieved. Confident. Relaxed. Curious. Yearning. Grateful. I actually *wanted* to go back. I wanted to approach my new laptop again.

This, of course, is evangelism at its finest. What could the Church learn from the Apple Store and Ryan? First, let's think about the slogan, *"I could talk about this stuff for hours."* What an amazing thought. Could we talk about our faith for hours? Are we passionate enough, knowledgeable enough, confident enough, and willing enough to talk about it for hours?

Next, do we know how to connect with people exactly where they are? I wasn't kidding when I said I needed a kindergarten teacher for my computer skills. And Brian, the greeter, knew exactly whom to call. When we encounter another person, especially a newcomer to our faith community, do we know how to meet that person where he or she is, no strings attached?

Ryan didn't sigh at me when I was exasperatingly slow. He didn't judge me for being hesitant. He didn't laugh when I called myself an old woman, hoping if I was self-abasing enough I could beat him to it. Each time I "got it," meaning I understood what he was showing me, I felt so relieved and happy. "Yes," I thought to myself. "Success."

Do we know whom to call if we don't know an answer? If we are sharing our spiritual journey with another and we can't answer a question or we aren't sure, do we know who and what our resources are? Rather than making up an answer or working around it, or perhaps even implying that the question was silly or stupid, will we do the work to find out the answer? Ryan wasn't apologetic when he was confused about something. He didn't change the subject to avoid the question. He simply said, "Let me find someone who might know more about this than I do." Imagine that.

I've been wondering what a "One-to-One" evangelism program might look like. Could we offer, like the Apple Store does, to sit with anyone who wants it, one-to-one, one hour a week for a year? Valuing questions rather than answers might evoke an entirely new energy in a church. What are your questions? Let's sit down once a week for a year and talk about your questions. You can bring any questions you have. We will not judge you or shame you. We will not try to fit you into a mold. Instead, we will listen to you, get to know you, and find out what you need. In the process, we will be willing to learn something new ourselves.

I end with a note about the store itself. The entire front of it is glass, street to roof. You can see everything that is going on—a concrete example of full transparency. It is streamlined and clean; there's not much to distract you from the process at hand. People seem to know why they are there. Very little pretense.

It's a transformational model.

DIGGING DEEPER

1. When you hear the word *evangelism*, what comes to your mind?

2. How might you share your faith journey with others? What would you feel comfortable sharing? What would make you feel uncomfortable?

3. What happens inside of you when you entertain new religious and theological ideas? Make a list of ten questions you have always wanted to ask but were either ashamed or embarrassed to ask. If you can summon the courage, share one of these questions with another or with a group.

4. What do you think it would be like to sit with another person for an hour a week in order to get to know them and for them to ask you questions about your faith? Can you imagine yourself doing this? If not, why not?

Talking with Strangers

I do not
Want to step so quickly
Over this sacred place on God's body
That is right beneath your own foot
As I
Dance with
Precious life
Today.
—Hafiz[24]

It was our third morning in a row at the coffee shop on the corner of Washington and Main Street, Providence, Rhode Island. On each day of our visit, we had enjoyed their egg-white flatbread sandwiches, along with a wonderful cup of coffee. But this third morning the staff had forgotten to make my sandwich without cheese and my coffee was lukewarm. A woman sitting a few tables down noticed me talking to my husband and pointing to my sandwich. She turned around and called kindly but firmly to the teenager behind the counter, "Anthony, fix this order. Customer service first."

Sylvie works taking and filling orders at this shop, but today she had just stopped in for a bite before boarding the bus for her job at the airport. She works seven days a week, five at the airport at a food kiosk and two here. Sylvie is a woman of mixed descent, Spanish and Lebanese. She has an endearing countenance, a bright and wide smile, soft olive skin, full cheeks, and the kind of dark eyes that seem to have no separation between the pupil and the brown part. Her voice has a musical cadence to it as she speaks.

We started an easy conversation about Providence, our visit, her jobs, her broken-down car. Then we talked a little about our families, toasted our mutual wedding anniversaries, and even talked about 9/11 and our common connections with New York City.

I cannot remember exactly when the conversation turned, but at some point she mentioned God, and how she counts her blessings every day and how she believes in the power of prayer. It seemed organic and natural for Sylvie to be sharing like this. It was like she was saying, "This is my life. This is who I really am. I can't not tell you." She wasn't asking me about my beliefs, she was just sharing hers. She wasn't trying to convince me of anything or even to assert her own convictions. She was just naturally and easily sharing something that was a vital part of her life.

I remember thinking, "This is evangelism, an invitation to enter Holy Ground." If I were a non-believer, Sylvie would have aroused my curiosity. Hmmm . . . here's a woman who's raised four decent children, works two jobs, helps with her grandchildren, took time to help me, and still has a compelling smile on her face and softness in her eyes. I could tell Sylvie's life was not easy, not full of earthly pleasure or financial independence. I could tell by her pitted sweater and worn-out shoes that new clothes and fashion are not high on her priority list. I got the feeling she didn't take vacations like the one we were taking, staying at a downtown hotel and spending time touring a city. But Sylvie was happy, secure in things longer lasting than immediate pleasure and financial gain. Sylvie was full of the peace and love of God. She was resting in the moment, thanking God for taking care of her and her family another day, helping another person out, enjoying her food, and readying herself for work.

Sylvie has challenged me. How do I naturally and organically share my faith? How easily do I talk with friends and strangers about my prayer life, my relationship with God? When was the last time I was out for coffee (or at a grocery store, department store, gas station, daycare, church) and casually shared with a total stranger my core beliefs, those things that get me through the day?

It didn't take more than ten minutes to feel a connection to this lovely woman. I have no idea what denomination she belongs to, if any, or if she attends church. I don't know if we worship the same way or call God by the same name. I don't know if she is gay or straight, Republican or Democrat, legal or illegal. What I do know is that Sylvie sees herself as a child of God and celebrates that in the moment. I think she saw me as a child of God and connected with me from that perspective. I know that she believes in the power of prayer and in the power of love. And I know that this short and simple conversation has stayed with me and encouraged me to think about how I talk with strangers.

Digging Deeper

1. How do you naturally and organically share your faith or core beliefs? With friends and family? With strangers? What beliefs do you hold that you wouldn't want to share? Can you state them clearly, at least to yourself?

2. How does it change the way you share if the person you are talking to has the same beliefs or faith as you do?

3. Why do you think people are shy about their beliefs?

4. It has been said that people at the same stage of faith development have more in common with those of other faiths than with those of their own faith who are at different stages of development. This could mean that a Christian and a Muslim might have more in common in terms of how they live their faith than two Christians or two Muslims might. What do you make of this concept? How have you experienced it?

Anything but the Kitchen Sink

Attention is a tangible measure of love. Whatever receives our time and attention becomes the center of gravity, the focus of our life. This is what we do with what we love: We allow it to become our center. What is the center of your life? Carefully examine where you spend your attention, your time. Look at your appointment book, your daily schedule.
—Wayne Muller[25]

We are doing a major renovation of our house. It'll be great when it's done, but in the meantime I've been living without a kitchen sink now for three months. There are other things we are living without: a washer and dryer, a dishwasher, stove, oven, books, TV, and any semblance of order. But the thing I miss most is the kitchen sink.

I was surprised. I didn't realize how much of my life revolves around the kitchen sink. Fill the coffee pot with water at the kitchen sink. Stir the cat food, rinse the spoon in the kitchen sink. Wipe the crumbs from the counter into the kitchen sink. Take my vitamins with a swig of water from the kitchen sink. Make a bowl of instant oatmeal with a cup of water from the kitchen sink. Throw the ice leftover in a glass in the kitchen sink. Make a salad, wash the cutting board in the kitchen sink. Cut my finger while opening mail, rinse and disinfect at the kitchen sink. Need a glass of water after working in the yard, go to the kitchen sink. Wash any dish, cup, glass, or pot or container in the kitchen sink. You get the idea.

I keep thinking about the saying, "She packed everything but the kitchen sink." I'm now thinking the kitchen sink should be the first thing to pack. We should pack the thing that our lives revolve around. I've never heard of the kitchen sink used as a metaphor for our relationship with God, and I'm wondering why not. My relationship with God is like my relationship with the kitchen sink. I stumble to this place first thing in the morning. I turn it on to start the process of nourishing myself. I return to it constantly, to dump messes, to wash off utensils, to prepare food and drink, to offer others hospitality, to wash my hands, and sometimes to nurse a wound. When my daughter was days and weeks old, I bathed her in it. I washed my mother's hair in it when she couldn't shower any more. I prefer it to be tidy, but that's not always the case. One thing is certain: that sink is, for me, Holy Ground.

Maybe your time at home doesn't revolve around the kitchen. Because I like to cook, and because no matter how I try to use other rooms, every visitor to my house ends up in my kitchen, my home life mostly takes place in my kitchen. Wherever your life is centered at home, try thinking about it as a metaphor for your relationship with God. You might find it curious, helpful, and enriching as I did. I guess some of your metaphors might be a little more techno savvy, like "My relationship with God is like my relationship with the TV . . . or like my relationship with the computer . . . or with video games. . . ." Or maybe it's something like "My relationship with God is like my time in the workshop . . . or like my time in the garden." Just play with the idea and see what you come up with. I know this for sure. My mother was right when she said you don't realize how important something is until you don't have it. I will never take my kitchen sink for granted again. And I will try not to let the metaphor get lost in the busyness of everyday living.

DIGGING DEEPER

1. What objects in your daily life would you not want to be without? Share this list in a group.

2. It is easy to take things for granted. Write a prayer of gratitude for all of the many material things in your life that you have come to rely on.

3. Think of a metaphor or simile that best describes your relationship with God.

   My relationship with God is like . . .

   My relationship with God is . . .

4. Imagine that you have died and your friends will bury you with three things that describe and define your life. What would those things be?

When the Veil is Thin

*There is a sacredness in tears. They are not the mark of weakness,
but of power. They speak more eloquently than ten thousand tongues.
They are the messengers of overwhelming grief, of deep contrition,
and of unspeakable love.*
—Washington Irving[26]

A small, struggling congregation rents space from another small struggling congregation. The group that owns the building worships on Sunday mornings and has a full-time minister, and the congregation that rents the space worships on Sunday evenings. Both congregations share another very part-time minister who is mostly working for free. He is ordained, but not in either of the denominations that he's serving. They are, however, all in full communion with each other. Because he serves both congregations, there is some overlap in his ministry and that has resulted in dialogue about worshiping together and perhaps even joining together. This would seem the natural thing to do, practical, good use of resources, synergistic. There has been an obstacle, however—the members of the evening church are almost exclusively gay and lesbian.

Recently the part-time minister died in a car accident. Both congregations were traumatized. They scrambled to come together to plan a meaningful funeral, and members of both congregations rushed to be of support to the minister's family—his wife and fourteen-year-old son. The higher-ups in three denominations came to town to participate in the funeral. Soon after they arrived, they jockeyed for positions and debated dogma. How would they celebrate communion? Who would lead? How would they vest? In the spirit of respect and ecumenism, they figured it out, focused on what was important, and created a funeral liturgy that drew the congregations together and comforted the family.

After the service, there was a covered-dish supper in the parish hall. Members of both congregations mixed, sitting at tables with each other, crying together, and telling stories about their dear friend and pastor. At one of those tables sat an older lady who usually sits in the back of the church on Sunday *mornings*. She sits in the back because the last few rows of pews are padded and that makes it easier on her aging body. Her pew is filled with her elderly friends. Next to her at the table today was a handsome, thirty-something gay man who worships with the *evening* congregation. He is fun and outgoing with an easy smile. He told great stories about their now dead friend. He stopped for a moment in the middle of one of these stories to comment on the chicken potpie.

"This is the best potpie I have ever tasted," he exclaimed with his mouth still full. "I've got to find out who made it and get the recipe."

"Well, young man, I made it. It's my mother's recipe; been around for ages."

"Can you give it to me? I'd love to make this for my mother's seventieth birthday party."

"If you come to church Sunday *morning*," the woman says, slowing as she says the word *morning*, " I'll give you the recipe."

"I'll be there," he promises.

"One ingredient a week," she tells him, and the whole table erupts in laughter.

In the sacred moments of life, those moments when the veil between heaven and earth is thin, we recognize that we are all the same. We who are one body share one bread and one cup.

We all love. We all grieve. We laugh and we cry. We celebrate our friends and families. We all bleed. Artificial separations are just that. Artificial. Perhaps we need them to help us feel safe. We use separations as ways of defining ourselves by our differences. I might say, "This is how I know myself. I am a white, heterosexual, middle-class, mainline, liturgical Christian. This is how I interpret Scripture. I feel safe when I am with others just like me." It is the human condition, I guess. Yet we are called to transcend our desire for sameness and not only reach out to people who are different but also to intentionally stand with them, next to them, touching them. We are called to feed the hungry, clothe the poor, and befriend the needy. We are also told that when two or three gather, the Spirit of our Living God is there as well. It doesn't say two or three just like me. It says two or three. When we break bread together, when we grieve, worship, and commune together, then we remember that we are one. We remember that we are all dust and to dust we shall return. We remember that life is short and we do not have time to tarry.

Now is the time to love. Now is the time to join. Now is the time to accept. Now is the time to transform. Now. Now. Now.

DIGGING DEEPER

1. When have you experienced a time when the veil has been thinned between heaven and earth? What do you think accounts for these times?

2. When are you more comfortable with those who are different from you? What differences are easier for you than others?

3. What would help you be willing to step out of your comfort zone?

4. When the veil is thin, it is easy for people to get emotionally hurt because their normal defenses are lowered. If you have had the experience of being hurt during these thin times, write about it or talk about it with a friend or a group. Have you ever hurt anyone else during a time like this? What was that like for you? Often these hurts happen at times like deaths and funerals, weddings, baptisms, sicknesses, and traumas.

5. Knowing that the veil can be thin at times, how do you think it should inform our behavior and etiquette? What guidelines do you use during these times?

III.

LOAFING WITH GOD:

TRANSFORMED BY SABBATH

---

*Jesus and his community cannot be grasped in small informa-
tional doses but only through unhurried, percolated time.*

—Frank Honeycutt[27]

My only understanding of Sabbath as a child came from the commandment, "Remember the Sabbath day, and keep it holy" (Exodus 20:8). I believed that meant to go to church on Sundays, the Sabbath. We did our chores on Saturday, so we didn't have much house or yard work to do on Sundays, but I had no real idea about Sabbath. I did homework if it needed doing and Mom was still cooking meals. When I was a teenager I went back to church Sunday evenings for youth group, and some Sundays I got to church at 9:00 a.m. and, other than grabbing lunch, I stayed there for basketball games, cheerleading practice, and then youth group. It was wonderful and holy busyness. It formed me, but it didn't teach me how to listen for God's movement in my life, or how to allow for the Mystery in my life, or how to discern and separate my ego from God's will. In other words, it didn't transform me.

During my training as a spiritual director, I learned about Sabbath, that practice of truly resting in God. One lecture I heard during these studies encouraged observing the Sabbath an hour a day, a day a week, a weekend a quarter, a week a year, and a month every five years. An hour a day, just to loaf with God. The idea of it astonished me. What would that look like? Would I just sit still and listen? Could I walk in the garden? Chop fresh herbs? Drink a glass of wine? Listen to music? The German Lutheran in me knows how to be effective, efficient, structured. We know how to work, we German Lutherans. In my three years of confirmation class I never heard about Martin Luther resting, only that he was busy and distraught and wrote ninety-five theses. Loaf? It seemed almost sacrilegious to rest.

I have learned the practice of Sabbath over time. Learning the art of listening for God in daily meditation and contemplative prayer was a wonderful start. As I silenced my busy mind and honestly asked to hear God's truth, wisdom, and reality, holy guidance began to change my life.

About three years into my Sabbath exploration I began to take silent retreats, sometimes only a day and sometimes a weekend. This time was filled with quiet walks, prayer, mindfulness, and time in the creative process. I would be graced with poems writing themselves and pieces of scripture coming into my consciousness. I spent time in scripture, learning the process of *lectio divina*, a way of reading scripture meditatively, not theologically or academically. I would let my body sing, dance, do yoga, or whatever it felt like it needed to do to open to the Holy. I would breathe more deeply, it seemed, and my body would find a new place of rest. I spent time in nature. Long walks on the beach or in the mountains, and watching the rising or setting of the sun and moon seemed to allow my own natural rhythm to return, to evolve. Sometimes I was alone. Sometimes I was with a friend.

Over the last fifteen years, what I have come to believe about the practice of Sabbath is that it is our natural, instinctive way of being. We are designed to return to our Source. Little children do it naturally. They play and then they rest, play and rest. I wish I had been taught to listen in a more concrete way as a child. I would have cherished learning a practice of silence. Listening for God instead of talking to God would have been great learning.

Some people have asked me, "When I am resting in God, what am I listening for?" Good question. It is hard to say without knowing your life's circumstances. Let me begin by reminding you that you are resting. That is all you are doing. You don't have to listen or speak. Resting is pure unto itself. However, if you are intentionally listening for the voice of God, especially if you are wishing to discern something, remember that listening is a personal experience and it begins with emptying, getting the ego and false desires out of the way. I have heard people say they hear a voice. I've never heard a voice but I've had words put into my consciousness. For example, after praying for months (thinking about, asking for God's help, crying) about a relationship that was damaged, the words that finally "came to me," not as clear words but more as a complete and whole thought, were: "It's okay for this to be over. Let it go. There's nothing more for you to do now."

Sometimes we are listening more for our own reality, or, said another way, listening for our own intuition about something. Taking time to rest, breathe, unplug, and detach allows us to hear ourselves. Our *Selves*, the God-seed in us. What does our inner wisdom have to say about something? Perhaps the answer is waiting within us and just needs time and space to find its way to the surface. When we give ourselves the gift of Sabbath, the opportunity to descend to our most personal depths is available, and very often, the answers we are seeking are right there.

For me, Sabbath is also an opportunity to pay closer attention to my dreams. I try to remember my dreams every day and often journal about the ones that stick with me long enough for me to get them written down. When I am taking intentional Sabbath, it seems my dreams are clearer, bigger, and in a way more intrusive. It is as if the Holy is finding another way to reach me. And in Sabbath, I have time to look anew at past dreams that I have written down but not spent sufficient time processing.

Sabbath is not only an invitation to rest in God. It is an invitation to reconnect with one's Self. ". . . the kingdom of God is within you," we are told in Luke 17:21. Perhaps, at the deepest level of resting and returning, there are no gaps to bridge; there is no separation.

Bricks and Mortar

If the doors of perception were cleansed, everything
would be seen as it is.
—William Blake[28]

I love HGTV. I love it so much I should probably give it up for Lent. I don't watch much TV, but when I get into bed at night or when I'm putting on my make-up, I usually catch at least a portion of a show. Candice Olson is my favorite designer, and in my fantasy world she will come and design a new master bedroom for me, a perfect blend of feminine and masculine elements. Studded leather headboards. Crystal lamps. Ahh . . . fantasy.

Recently the show that has caught my attention is *Holmes on Homes*. It features a big Alpha-male, Mike Holmes, who goes around and rebuilds what other builders have ruined. "Mighty Mouse, to the rescue," I always want to shout in the background when he shows up. He goes way overboard, according to my husband's value engineering sensibilities. "Overkill," my husband grumbles.

Today's episode was a story about bricks being laid incorrectly. Not only had the mortar rotted, but the bricks themselves were crumbling. I found myself very curious. Mascara in hand, I turned around to watch more closely. The sturdiest of building blocks should surely stand up to anything, I thought. Yet given certain conditions, the right amount of dripping rain or snow, poor circulation or poor drainage, they crumble. The bricks on this show had eroded into pieces, pebbles and parts. The mortar, too, designed to hold these bricks together in a certain shape or foundation, had crumbled. The wall was so disintegrated that Mr. Holmes could stick his finger right into it. Oh my. I had to resist the urge to run outside and check our bricks and mortar.

As with the building of foundations, the technique is the key. The very way the bricks are laid and glued into place will determine durability. In between each brick, the mortar has to be slightly concave to repel anything dangerous that might stick. The enemy, weather, will find no purchase if the mortar is hollowed out just to a certain degree.

And so I think it is with us. Even the sturdiest, most resilient ones will crumble and crack given the right conditions. We must all hollow ourselves, have a place that is deeper, harder to touch, protected from the world. Our foundations must be laid properly. It's not enough for the raw material to be firm and tough. It has to be put together masterfully. The glue, it seems, must be concave, hollow, deeper than the parts it is holding together.

I wrote a poem in 2005 after my father spent twenty-one days in the hospital due to a staph infection. This is one of the verses I wrote:

> Or maybe his soul went
> in and in and in
> until it was safe from the
> assault of
> needles, scalpels, tubes and inserts,
> deep enough to fend off
> the attack,
> long enough to discern into which
> world it would travel next.

Recently I heard the phrase "go in and in" again, used in a poem by Danna Faulds:

> Go in and in.
> Be the space between two cells, the vast resounding silence in which spirit dwells.[29]

Like the mortar, we must go in and in. In to those places the world cannot touch. Into the places protected from the elements of weather and conditions. It is not easy to go in and in. It takes time. Time to be silent. Time to listen. Time away from the pull of everyday life. It takes courage. We do not always know what we will find deep in. Do we want to find out what we are really made of? It takes the realization that our bricks will crumble if we don't go in to the concave place, into the hollowness, into that place where the Holy One draws us. In and in, until, in our human hollowness, we find the Divine and the Divine imprint, solidly holding us together. The kingdom of God is within us.

DIGGING DEEPER

∞

1. What helps you become silent? What ways do you hollow or empty yourself to make room for the Divine?

2. Think about a period in your life that required you to pull "in and in and in." An illness? A deep grief? What did you experience during this time? How did friends experience you?

3. What are the components of your psycho/spiritual foundation? What beliefs, priorities, and practices do you rest upon?

4. What is the glue for your foundation? What holds it all together? In what times of life has your glue been truly tested?

Chimes

It all depends on how we look at things, and not on how things are in themselves. The least of things with a meaning is worth more in life than the greatest of things without it.

—C. G. Jung[30]

The sound of the wind is different these days, thanks to our new set of wind chimes. We bought them at the Abbey Press store in Meinrad, Indiana, home of the Archabbey of Meinrad. The day we visited, the sky was clear and blue, and it was sweater weather—just a hint of spring in the air. A few daffodils dotted the landscape and bushes had buds just ready to bloom. As we toured the campus, we were charmed by what looked and felt like a medieval town. A March breeze blew gently on the hill of this Abbey, and the wind chimes on the campus were in constant motion. We heard many high-pitched flute-like chimes, but we also heard deep chimes that sounded like Tibetan drums. It seemed the whole campus was wrapped in ringing chimes and we loved it. So, while at the Abbey's gift shop, we auditioned many sets of chimes. All were specially tuned and each had its own personality, from the long, thick, deep bass chimes to the slender and small soprano ones. We chose the tenor chimes because they sounded like the cello, one of my favorite instruments. Once home, we hung them just outside our porch.

Saturday morning, while I was enjoying my first cup of coffee on our screened-in porch, a soft breeze caught the chimes and they rang. There was something about the initial stillness on the porch and then the sudden ringing that heightened my senses. I immediately smiled, shut my eyes, and began to pray. I realized, even in the moment that it happened, that my quickly shutting my eyes and entering into prayer had been an almost reflexive response to the chimes, but I allowed myself to continue in my meditation and devotion. However, when I opened my eyes, I was curious about my response and I gave myself the luxury of sitting still and thinking about this.

I remembered a teacher telling me a story about his time at a monastery. He recalled that every time a bell rang, the monks on the campus dropped whatever they were doing and headed for the chapel. The monks who were gardening took off their gloves, shook off their clothes, and headed for the chapel. The monks who were cooking put their knives down, washed their hands, turned off the stove, and headed for the chapel. The monks who were cleaning wrung out their mops, wiped their hands on their aprons, and came to the chapel.

The bell was a reminder that it was time to come pray, and with near Pavlovian reflexes, all the monks responded in the same way. Hear the bell, head for the chapel.

Both my office and my house are located close to churches. For the past fifteen years, I have heard church bells ringing during the day. Some of them just chime, and occasionally others play a familiar tune or hymn. I notice them every time they ring, and I often say a silent prayer when I hear them. Sometimes it is nothing more than, "I know you are there, God," or "O Holy One, thank you." On Saturday, when I heard my new wind chimes, I realized that over the course of many years I have learned to use the sound of a bell to think instantaneously about all that is holy and good and to give thanks. It has happened almost unconsciously, certainly subtly, but it has happened. And I realized how much I enjoy that response. I like having a frequent reminder to interrupt myself and tune back in to the abundance, purity, and holiness that are always available to us.

What are your daily reminders? A friend told me she puts a verse from a psalm on her dashboard to help her remember to slow down and breathe. Some people use the beginning of a meal, if only for a moment, to be grateful for the creation. Another friend told me she tapes a word or a phrase to her bathroom mirror, changing it every so often as she is working on something or learning about something. A daily delve into scripture or a special prayer might help.

A client told me recently that her grandmother's cross, which she never takes off, is her reminder to stay tuned into God. "I find myself holding this cross frequently during the day, as if God can come through this piece of jewelry to my heart." Art can be a reminder. A carefully placed icon or painting that speaks to you about your relationship with the Holy can remind you to pause and remember who we are and whose we are. In our living room we have a large framed print of Rembrandt's *The Prodigal Son*. This painting is important to my husband. He loves this bible story and says that for him the painting is a constant reminder of God's unconditional love and mercy. I have friends who prefer the garden as their reminder. They say that a daily walk in the garden reminds them of the power of the Creator.

We all have to find our own ways to stay tuned-in to the Holy and to enjoy moments of daily Sabbath. Like toddlers returning to a parent's leg for just a moment of support, we can return again and again to the side of the Holy One. It is easy, very easy, to go through our busy days and forget what is most real. Having a sacred reminder is a practical way to re-member yourself (your *Self*) . . . to transform the fragmented Self into the wholeness and holiness you are meant to be.

DIGGING DEEPER

1. What symbols, sights, or sounds in your life help you to slow down and pay attention to the Holy? If you don't already have a visual or auditory reminder, think about something that might work.

2. What poem or scripture verse is particularly close to your heart? Consider sharing that with someone else and telling them why that means so much to your spiritual life.

3. An icon is something that when you look at it, you see the face of God, you see the Holy Other. It can be a picture, painting, or even a person. There are traditional icons from Orthodox religions, but an icon can be anything through which you see God's face. What or who are the icons in your life?

The Necessity of Silence

*One's effort is to be silent enough to hear, first the deepest needs
of one's own heart, and then the prompting of the creative Spirit
in whatever direction it may indicate.*
—Morton Kelsey[31]

We've all had them. Those weeks when the world seems too full
of suffering, too full of hatred, too full of complications and
questions that appear to have no answers. Recently I had one
of those weeks, and I am still struggling today, wishing my spirit
had more lightness, wishing I could feel as great as the day looks.
It is a clear and sunny spring day, and the buds of spring are
beginning to burst.

In Illinois, a young, promising graduate student opened fire on
fellow students, killing six and traumatizing an entire community.
In New York City, a therapist was murdered with a meat cleaver in
her private practice office by a man who was unhappy with treatment he had received some years ago. She wasn't even the one
who treated him, not that it really matters. A colleague confides in
me that more and more of the young adult/college-age population
he treats have clinical psychosis, a loss of contact with reality. A
friend's brother completes suicide. A neighbor's child is diagnosed
with a malignant tumor.

What is happening? Certainly I do not claim to have any hold
on the complexities of the world. But I do relate to a sermon I
read recently. Entitled "The Walrus of the Living God," it was
preached on January 8, 2008 by Maggie Ross, an Anglican solitary

and author residing in the United Kingdom. In this sermon, Ms. Ross suggests that not only is the ecology of our planet Earth out of balance, but the ecology of our souls is in severe disarray as well. She states plainly and simply that our souls require silence. Our souls were designed to be in silence and are finely tuned when they experience their core silence.

Now that may give us a clue about what is wrong. At least it's a sliver of an answer to a problem that feels bottomless, like a black hole. Silence. I am not saying that silence is a cure for mental illness, although I can imagine that a calmer life might help those suffering with such illnesses. Some silence might help us make better choices, might slow down the impulsivity of our choices. Some silence, some entering into the Heart of our heart, could reestablish the balance between what is real and personal and what is being projected onto others.

If you are an urban or suburban dweller, when was the last time you had real silence? A client told me recently that her home lost power for several hours. The "silence," she reported, was almost overpowering. The refrigerator wasn't humming, the HVAC wasn't cranking up, the TV wasn't making background noise, the home phone wasn't ringing, the fluorescent light in her kitchen was quiet. Total silence. *Weird at first*, she thought, and then a bit uncomfortable. Even outside the house, where only the sounds of nature were present, was silent. But as the hours wore on, she settled in, lit some candles, and let herself feel the gift of a few silent hours. "Balm for my soul," she said.

If you are younger than forty, when was the last time you experienced silence? Most of the people who would fit into this category know about being plugged in. The cell phone is always on, and "texting" is a 24/7 activity. Many high school and college kids I know sleep with their phones next to them in bed, and receive texts and phone messages throughout the night. Even sleep isn't silent any more. And waking? In addition to cell phones, there are iPods, iPads, computers, radios, televisions, video games, PDAs, busy malls, and the like to keep us eternally plugged in. Where is the room for silence?

If we are to experience God's reality, I believe we must *make* room for it. If our brains are constantly bombarded with noise, the ecology of our souls will begin to disintegrate. We are designed to know ourselves and to know God through the silence of the soul. Dare I say that in our silence we have the opportunity to remember who God is and remember who we are?

How do we fight the cultural norm of noisiness? We could turn off the TV, radio, iPod, and computer, maybe for just a thirty-minute period. Even eating dinner without any accompanying noise could be a beginning. We could try sitting in silence for ten minutes a day, doing nothing but paying attention to our breath. Better yet, visiting a garden, park, or green space to help us stay attuned to the natural world might silence our inner chatter and reestablish in us a sense of the order of creation. Would our schools be willing to offer a period of silence, maybe just five minutes at a time? Could those of us in churches ask for longer periods of silence? How could we teach our youth the value of silence? Of contemplation? Of listening?

We must be willing to give up the familiar noise and risk that we might encounter when we become silent. My own experience with silence is that it will bring questions and it will bring answers. It will bring suffering and it will bring hope. It will challenge me and it will soothe me. Like anything that is real, it will be paradoxical. When we touch the heart of God through practiced silence, nothing will remain the same. That is the fear and that is the hope. When Augustine said, "Without God, we cannot; without us, God will not," I think he knew the critical importance of communing with God through silence. Perhaps it is one way to start making real changes.

DIGGING DEEPER

1. What does the experience of silence evoke in you?

2. Where and when is it easiest for you to be silent? Indoors? Outdoors? At the ocean? In the mountains? Sitting still? Moving? Alone? Accompanied?

3. For two minutes, notice your breathing without judging it. Just close your eyes and follow your breath in and out. Is it deep? Shallow? Smooth? Jerky? Warm? Cool? What happens to you when you just notice your breath?

4. Have you ever kept intentional silence in a group? This could mean ten minutes of silence or days of silence, intentionally held by a specific group. How would you describe that experience? If you have never had that experience, would you be willing to try it? Why or why not?

5. Simon and Garfunkel recorded a song called "The Sound of Silence." Find of copy of that song and listen to it. Try sharing it in a group setting.

Loafing with God

I am too full.
I am full of things that block out
Your golden grace.
I am smothered by gods of my own creation
I am lost in the forest of my false self
I am full of my own opinions and narrow attitudes
full of fear, resentment, control
full of self pity, and arrogance.
I am so full, there is no room for you.
—Macrina Wiederkehr[32]

Preparing to enter thirty-six hours of silence at Kanuga Camp and Conference Center in Hendersonville, North Carolina, I cried my way through these words, part of a longer meditation entitled "Prayer of the Empty Water Jar" by Macrina Wiederkehr.

Knowing that this extended silence has come for me at a perfect time, I am holding on to the words I heard at a recent lecture. "Spend some time loafing with God." It is not something I do very often. Oh, I pray, meditate, do yoga, walk labyrinths, read, and even spend lengths of time in silence. But loaf? Do nothing? I can feel my German blood curdling right now at the thought of being—what? Lazy? The worst sin, right up there with whining. Perhaps I can rest in God. I do allow myself to rest. Relax with God. Let God support me. I am trying all kinds of rewrites to not have to loaf with God. This is the first morning.

On my walk to the dining hall this first silent morning, something caught my eye—the base of what once was a large pine tree.

It was about five feet in diameter with a hole in the center so large that there was more hole than tree. Growing out of the hole was a mass of light green, mossy lichen. I peered into the hole to see how the plant was growing, where it was coming from. All I could tell was that it was coming right up through the middle of the hole of the used-to-be pine tree.

God, if I empty myself like that pine tree and create a hole right in the middle of me, will you fill it with something that vibrant and beautiful? If I am no longer who I am now, will you make me something else? Can I become a container for a new creation to grow? And God, what if you are like the hole? Right out of the middle of you, God, a new creation is forming. What if I could be a part of that?

Perhaps with a little more loafing I can make the space to find out.

Later in the day I focused on these words from Wiederkehr's meditation:

> Finally,
> I sit with my empty water jar
> I hear you whisper
> You have become a space for God
> Now there is hope
> Now you are ready to be a channel of Life.
> You have given up your own agenda
> There is nothing left but God.

I am beginning to have a new appreciation of loafing with God. I am beginning to think about Jesus. In the end, Jesus was a complete container for God. In the end, there was nothing left but God. This silence, this loafing, has helped me remember my own desire to be a container for God. Such irony, that in doing nothing, the most important something happened. My desire for God returned.

DIGGING DEEPER

1. In what ways are you too full for God? What do you need to clear out to make room for God?

2. Try this simple way of emptying prayer: Sit comfortably with your hands cupped in your lap, palms up. Let your intention be to become aware of those things that keep you cluttered, too full for God. As they come into awareness, name them and put those things one at a time into your cupped hands. Then lift your hands up over your head and release it to God. When you feel done, just sit in silence for a few moments. You can return to this practice anytime you wish.

3. We are a culture addicted to busyness. What are the consequences for you personally of being too busy? What do you see as the cultural consequences of our busyness?

4. What are the positive qualities to being busy? Name them.

5. It has been said that the cure for burnout isn't necessarily rest but wholeheartedness. How would you know if you were busy in a wholehearted way or just busy?

When Others Pray For Us

In music, we may taste with wonder, though never comprehend,
the wisdom of God.
—Dr. Albert Blackwell[33]

I knew it would be close. 5:26 p.m. I raced out of my office, put my lipstick on at a traffic light, did a U-turn into the Goodyear parking lot, ran across the street, took the stairs two at a time, and slipped into a seat in the back of Avery Hall, Trinity Cathedral, Columbia, South Carolina. Choral evensong for Epiphany had already started, and the psalm, I think, was being sung as I took a few deep breaths and unzipped my winter coat. A friend slipped in next to me and a few other stragglers hurried in behind us as well. I made it. I'm here. Please, dear God, let me really be present, I prayed. I need an hour of Sabbath time.

I had been up to my ears that week in client crises. Nine straight hours of client contact the day before and seven that day plus a two-hour meeting. It's not unusual for this time of year. People tend to put their emotional issues on the shelf just to "get through the holidays." Then, holidays over, down they come and out they pour. Although it was only midweek, I was already feeling weary, working hard to stay grounded, centered, and open, a channel for the work God is doing in others' lives. I had trouble praying earlier that day. Evensong was calling.

It is hard to describe the pure joy and grace it was for me that Epiphany evening to have a choir praying and singing for me. For Episcopalians, and in most liturgical churches, worship, and especially the Eucharist, is active. One reads, sings, responds, intercedes, stands up, sits down, kneels, and greets others. No wonder the comedian Robin Williams refers to all this action as pew aerobics.

I probably wouldn't have gone that night if the service being offered would have required that much activity from me. I wanted to sit down and breathe. I wanted to hear someone else sing "My soul doth magnify the Lord" and "Lord, now lettest thou thy servant depart in peace." I wanted to sit silently and hear the earthly angels intercede for me. I was more than willing to let the monastics, in this case the choir, do their job of upholding the rest of us with their prayers.

I have had friends and family tell me that even in a state of unconsciousness, they have felt and "known" somehow that others were praying for them. Recently a client called me from his hospital room, just days after coming out of a medically induced coma, to say that although he had not been able to communicate, he had felt the presence of prayers and of the Holy Spirit. He "knew" that a clergy group he belonged to had been holding him in prayer, and he had "attached himself" to that awareness during the time of the coma and in the weeks following.

I have felt the power of the prayer of others. When my daughter had serious surgery, I truly felt bathed in prayer for days on end. It felt a bit like being under water, held in the safety of a marine-cocoon. When our family experienced the deaths of a best friend and beloved teacher, my mother, and my brother-in-law in just days, again I felt carried by prayer. But this time I didn't feel like I was under water in a cocoon. This time I experienced the sensation of support as being underneath me, as if I was buoyed from below and could trust that support. There were times during the day when I imagined myself floating on my back, floating on a river of prayer.

My personal experience of being prayed for has made me consider what prayer might mean on a more global level. When there are crises like earthquakes, typhoons, floods, wars, geno-cide, plague, or famine, I now believe that the prayers of all peo-ple and nations matter and are needed. If we are not face-to-face with the tragedy, our distant prayers may not seem to be use-ful. But my own experiences have convinced me of the power of prayer. Prayer is not the least we can do; it may be the most we can do. When disaster strikes, we can and must send money, supplies, and people. But even that is not enough. We must hold all countries and suffering people in our prayers. We can stay aware of the suffering and poverty and pray that God will be made known to all those who are there. We must pray, because we remember those times when we were too weary to pray for ourselves, and the prayers of others held us, carried us, and strengthened us. We don't have to understand why this works; we can just do it.

At Evensong last week, I was able to let the choir and the beau-tiful music they made carry me, pray for me, lift me up, and hold me. I could let God pray in me, my only job being to open myself to that grace and love. I did not have to do anything but be pres-ent and open. A Sabbath moment seized me. Many thanks to our musicians, who not only make beautiful music, but who pray for us, open the way for our own prayers to surface, and serve as our channels for God to pray in us.

I awoke the next morning with the old Paul Simon song "Like a Bridge Over Troubled Water" playing in my mind. "Like a bridge over troubled water, I will lay me down." It certainly says some of what I was feeling that night as the choir laid themselves down for me so that I could experience Sabbath.

DIGGING DEEPER

1. What has the experience of being prayed for felt like to you? How did you notice it?

2. How do you pray for others? The nations of the world? What do you think is happening when you and others pray? How would you describe this to someone new to faith?

3. What image or a metaphor would you use to describe how you feel when you are being held in prayer? You could be creative with this by writing a poem or painting a picture of this.

4. If you are in a small group, try making a living sculpture that would depict someone being held in prayer.

IV.

FAMILY, FRIENDS, AND COMMUNITY:

TRANSFORMED BY OTHERS

I tell you, families are definitely the training ground for forgiveness. At some point you pardon the people in your family for being stuck together in all their weirdness, and when you can do that, you can learn to pardon anyone. Even yourself, eventually.

—Anne Lamott[34]

The late Shaun McCartey, S.T. (1929–2007), was one of the instructors in my spiritual director's training program. A bit like a leprechaun, Shaun could be whimsical, weaving children's books and wonderful stories throughout his lectures. He read us *Wilfrid, Gordon, McDonald Partridge*, by Mem Fox, as a way of illustrating spiritual memory. And Daniel Pinkwater's *Doodleflute* taught the concept of friendship, abundance and scarcity. Perhaps my favorite, Mark Karlin's *Music Over Manhattan*, took the listener on a divine journey as a little boy found his true vocation. Even though his talks were instructional and deep, I never felt overwhelmed or confused, even after the most difficult material was presented.

Shaun wrote a book entitled *Partners in the Divine Dance of Our Three-Person'd God*. In this book, and in his lecture on relationships, he used the concept of God being in relationship with God-self. I am not sure exactly why, but that day, more than any previous time, I had a felt sense of the mystery of the Trinity. I also began to have words and an image for something near and dear to my heart: human relationship.

This is the image that formed in my mind nearly sixteen years ago. Imagine, if you can, concentric circles. The center circle holds you and God. In the next circle are your parents. Then your immediate family, if you have siblings. Next your extended family, grandparents, aunts and uncles, and cousins. After that is your local community, which might include your neighborhood, your schools, your faith community, groups like Boy Scouts and Girl Scouts. Further out, still, would be the culture in which you grew up, and way out might be the decade in which you were born and what was going on in the world at that time. Overarching, surrounding, and penetrating the entire set of concentric circles is God, and a God who is already in relationship with God-self.

In each of these concentric circles, we have relationships. In the innermost circle, our relationship is with our Source or Creator. Here we are raw and untouched. The Creator is our first and primary relationship, the place where we are our most authentic selves, untouched by this thing we call living. The next circle, the first circle in which we live in this world, is the relationship with our parents. This relationship begins to shape us from the time of our very conception. We are welcomed, or not. We are safe, or not. We are supported, or not. We are nurtured, or not. We learn how to love and be loved, or not. We are taught how to give and how to receive, or not. We are valued, or not. We are forgiven, or not. With our parents and families we begin to learn about the rules of relationships and about the love in relationships. We have all experienced the impact of family on forming us and transforming us.

Our extended families, our communities, and our circumstances continue to form and transform us. As we choose friends, faith communities, and social communities, we continue to be changed and shaped. The extent to which each of these relationships helps us become the most authentic self we can become is the extent to which the relationship reminds us of who we were originally created to be, and therefore mirrors our relationship with God and God's relationship with God-self. The more relationships teach us that we are safe, nurtured, supported, valued, and celebrated, the more they mirror our relationship with God. When family and community call upon us to live in love, to be our authentic selves, to be sacrificial, to give of ourselves for others, to empty ourselves for the good of the whole, the more we are being transformed into the image of God. When relationships and communities yield the fruits of the spirit—patience, hope, kindness, truthfulness, peace, joy, and self-control—the more they mirror God's relationship with the God-self.

The One who exists in relationship created us to be in relationship. We are made in that image. It is in these earthly relationships that we are formed. It is also in these relationships that we can be *transformed* back into the original wholeness that was meant to be.

Immigrant Hearts

The heart that breaks open can contain the whole universe.
—Joanna Macy[35]

I am the child of an immigrant, and I married the child of an immigrant. I have come to learn over time that there is a place in all the immigrants I know, a place so deep as to almost be cellular, that I think of as the immigration wound. It is not a visible wound, like a surgery scar. But if you grow up as the child of an immigrant, or you spend enough time with one, you learn that the wound is there. You have to piece the cues together over years, though. There are the sayings. "Nothing matters but family." "You have no idea how lucky you are." "I wish you knew my grandparents."

More elusive than the sayings, but more telling, are the emotions of remembrance. The tears. Every Christmas Eve, while singing "Silent Night" in German. Every time my extended family gathers for a meal and a blessing is said, thanking God for bringing all of us *together* safely. Each time slides are shown or pictures of the Old Country come out of hiding. There is the deep laughter, too, and what feels like pure joy, when celebrations include the culture of the left country. Homemade sauerkraut and wurst, beer and German potato salad. Polkas and umpa bands. Laughter, ruddy cheeks, and sparkling eyes.

The language might even change then. A phrase here and there. Words, *"liebchen, tochter, aber schön,"* spoken from a deep place, reaching for home.

I believe my deep desire, indeed my vocation, to tend hearth, gather family and friends, create community, and treasure diversity comes, at least in part, from being the child of an immigrant. The wound that holds the feelings of leaving, of separation, of loss, of confusion, of fragility and being different, of striving to fit in, that is the wound that I watched and tended growing up.

When it was time for my siblings and me to pick a college, my father insisted we go to one at least 500 miles away. He wanted us to have our own immigration, to leave what was comfortable and familiar, to see other lands, to meet other people, to learn how to live with and work with a broader cross-section of life. I left New York to attend Furman University in Greenville, South Carolina in 1974. It was a difficult migration for me, fraught with misunderstanding, loneliness, foreign food, strange religions, and odd habits.

In so many ways, that move was harder and stranger than my five-month stay in Japan. I expected things to be very different halfway across the world and in a very foreign country. But the migration South had so many unexpected challenges. At home in Melville, Long Island, I was considered fairly conservative, a good girl, and that was my perception of myself as well. But at Furman, I was seen as liberal and loose. My halter tops and hip-hugger jeans were frowned upon by many of the more conservative students. When I suggested going out for pizza and beer, I was immediately added to the Campus Crusade for Christ's prayer list. I found this out because a note appeared on my bedroom door, letting me know I was on the list. My freshman boyfriend and I had to sneak into the bell tower to make out because watchful and judging eyes were everywhere on the campus. And although this has nothing to do with being liberal or conservative, and as superficial as it may seem, eating was a challenge. I really missed many foods. Bagels. Hard salami. Rye bread. Pastina. Crunchy vegetables. New York Cheesecake.

But in that foreign land, I have made my home. Because my siblings and I all had to leave New York and pick a college in another part of the country, I have siblings in North Carolina, Chicago, and Dallas. I have an only daughter who has made her way to New York and I wonder, "Is it in the blood, this leaving home and going away?" So, like my father who missed his home and his family, I miss mine too, all the time.

Paradoxically, when we all get together, it usually feels like too much for me. Too much happiness, sadness, noise, celebration. Too much catching up. Not enough time. Quiet time. Easy time. Time I see other families get who live close to each other. Stopping in for a quick chat. Sunday lunch. Worship together. Shopping. Swimming. Hunting. Care-taking. Hugs.

I love to create quiet, easy time. Deep time. I do this for a living. I do it for my soul's need. I am at my happiest when I am with family and close friends. I especially like to do this in my home where I can cook wonderful food for people, play beautiful music, engage in healing conversations, and remember how connected we all are. This is healing balm for those wounds of loneliness and immigration.

I believe we all have our wounds of immigration. We have all had many kinds of leaving that we could recount if we gave ourselves a moment to think about it. Those leavings, as much as they may hurt, also form, direct, and remind us that we must take our home with us. Wherever we are, what truly matters we must carry within us.

What if we thought about our birth as our initial immigration, leaving our place with the Holy to be here on this earth as humans? We all feel it, that hunger to return to our natural state of union with the Divine. We all feel the loneliness, the disconnect, the deep yearning. Can we tend *that* hearth and invite the Holy Other in, spending some time with the Source of our Eternal Home to heal our loneliness?

When she was four years old, my daughter called to me from her bedroom. She seemed close to sleep, in a dreamlike state. She looked drowsy, her eyes half shut, her jaw slightly slack. Her breathing was slow, and her voice was just a whisper.

"Momma, where was I before I was with you?"

"Where do you think you were, Sweetie?"

"I think I was with God."

"And so you were," I said, kissing her goodnight and stroking her hair until her eyes shut fully.

I tend to my family, friends, and community, and, as I do so, I tend to the Holy Other. This tending has formed and transformed me. Truly, nothing makes me happier.

DIGGING DEEPER

∞

1. Who do you long to see but do not? What does this longing feel like? What color or shape is this longing? Where do you feel it in your body?

2. What places in your life call to you? The beach? The mountains? A big city? A certain part of our country or a certain country? How are these places related to a feeling of home? Safety? Belonging?

3. What do you believe about your soul? How do you experience your soul as being connected to God day to day? If your soul longs for God, how do you feel this longing? In what ways do you respond to it?

4. If there were a heaven that could be filled with the things that make you feel most at home, what things would be there?

5. Sometimes the word "vocation" has a spiritual implication. Really, it just means who you are most authentically in the world. With this in mind, how has your childhood family system shaped your vocation?

Reunion

Love, like a carefully loaded ship
crosses the gulf between the generations. . . .
We live, not by things, but by the meanings of things.
It is needful to transfer the passwords
from generation to generation.
—Antoine de Saint Exupéry[36]

Every other year, my extended family (parents, siblings, spouses, significant others, and children) gathers for a week at the beach. I haven't kept an accurate account, but I remember a few gatherings before I had my soon-to-be twenty-five-year-old daughter, so I think we've been at this for about thirty years. Fifteen reunions.

I stopped calling them vacations about a decade ago. Even though it might be the only week I had off during the summer, calling it vacation made me a little nuts. When you come home from a week at the beach exhausted to the point of tears and call that vacation, it just messes with your head. Terming it *reunion* made my tears and exhaustion more justified.

Most years I would come home and wonder why we keep doing this. Please hear this: I love and respect my family. I enjoy each of my three siblings and their spouses. We travel to see each other many times in between reunions. I adore my nieces and nephews. But gathering anywhere from seventeen to twenty-five people in one place and trying to be together for a week simply unglues me. When the seven children were preschool age, we had a difficult week together. That's a euphemism for the fact that we were driving each other crazy. My older sister and her husband wanted to keep the kids up late so that they would sleep late in the morning. My husband and I wanted the kids down early so we could have some adult time at night. My father insisted the kids eat everything put on their plates. My brother's kids didn't eat much of anything, and weren't going to start that week. Matthew, age two, bit Michael, age three, right on the cheek, just minutes before we were going to have family pictures taken. My mother stayed in her bedroom most of the week because she couldn't stand the noise. If this was vacation, I wanted nothing more to do with it. Apparently, neither did my other sibs, so we put our creative juices together. We love each other and we want to see each other. We want the cousins to get to know each other and enjoy each other. We brainstormed possibilities for a few days and decided for the next reunion we would get a few side-by-side condos instead of one big house. That helped. A lot. We would gather in a different condo each evening for dinner, and we would eat out a couple of nights, too.

Even after several years of side-by-side condos, my family continues to have its difficulties. Herding cats is an accurate description of any attempt to move my family in one direction at the same time. Everyone has a different understanding of time and of being on time. One year after piling in cars and caravanning around Hilton Head trying to find a restaurant that could seat us, a nephew suggested that we could star in a reality show entitled "Twenty Idiots on an Island." Perfect. Even so, it felt important to visit and to watch the cousins begin to love and play with each other. I especially enjoyed extra time with my two brothers, one who lives in Dallas and the other in Chicago. Because I see them less, I made a point of spending time lingering over morning coffee, taking long walks on the beach, or sharing a glass of wine after we got all the kids to bed. But despite the many joys, I still came home utterly exhausted.

My father has never understood my ambivalence about this week. He is an immigrant. He knows the pain of families divided, and he luxuriates in his family's being together. Standing with his hands on his hips like the king of Siam, he sighs, "It doesn't get any better than this," and smiles at me.

"It does for me, Dad," I say. I've explained to him that I "do" relationships for a living, and that being in close quarters for a week and trying to "do" relationships with every family member just about puts me over the edge. I want to do it. I believe it's important. It just exhausts me.

This year we topped our numbers with twenty-five people. The "kids" (eight cousins) range in age from thirteen to twenty-five now. They all came and many brought their significant others. Two came all the way from California, and one niece's boyfriend came from Denver just to meet the family. They all *wanted* to come. "I wouldn't miss it. It's so important. It's family." These are the words they say when I thank them for coming from such a long distance, for taking off of work or school, for bringing their friends. I thank the visitors. I say, "You're brave. It's not easy joining this family for a week." They say, "It's great. You guys are fun. I wish my family got together like this."

One evening, while sitting on the couch with my sibs and watching the now-"grown" cousins and their friends squished hip to hip around a table, laughing and playing a game of Apples to Apples, I thought, "Look what we created. Cousins who love each other and want to be together. A deep sense of family that transcends our culture's devaluing of it. I can see the fruits of our labor. I am so grateful." My father had given a beautiful speech the night before. He reminded us all of how blessed we are and repeated his life-long mantra: "Nothing is more important than family." He said he thought our family had two important qualities, Strength and Unity. He was right on both accounts. He and my mother modeled and required that of us. I had the distinct sense that she was with us in that room, contented. I also knew in that moment that the experience of family had formed and trans-formed all of us.

When I was growing up, I didn't see my cousins every other year. They lived in Florida; we lived in New York. We didn't gather and stay connected. It wasn't something we had the time or money to do. So watching this living piece of art unfold this past week was, for me, Holy Ground. I had the sense that all of those years of hanging in there, finding creative ways to make it easier, honoring each other's needs, respecting each person's uniqueness, being honest, and just showing up because it was important, have created something that is enduring, something that matters.

I don't think I can call it "vacation" yet. For me vacation involves silence, reading, and very few personal or time commit-ments. But when I say "reunion" two years from now, I think it will reverberate within me in a new and different way.

DIGGING DEEPER

1. What in your life have you stuck with even though you wondered why you kept doing it? What were the fruits of that persevering attitude? Were there any outcomes that were problematic? Any regrets?

2. We all know that families can be tough. How have you been creative in staying connected with family, even through the difficult times? Have you been creative in setting boundaries? In prayer? In conversation? In rituals? In gift-giving?

3. "Pick your battles." This is a common instruction given to new parents and new partners. In your family, what battles have you had to let go of? Which ones are worth fighting? How has this helped or hurt the family's relationship?

4. What do you think about my father's statement, "Nothing is more important than family"? How has your connection to family transformed you?

5. Some people need time and distance to heal from abusive or toxic families. Reunions, visits, even phone calls can be traumatic. If you fall into this category, do you have friends or a community that substitute as family for you? How do you stay connected? What are your rituals?

Leaning on Friends

I am leaning on my friends like the arms of Jesus
How they hold me up.
—Tom Conlon[37]

My client has a graduate degree in counseling. She works full time for a state agency and has been there for five years. Because of various budget cuts, overtime cuts, program cuts, and health insurance premium increases, her salary is less than it was several years ago. Once she pays her bills (she has no credit card debt but does have some school loans), she has $200 left for gas, food, and miscellaneous expenses. Every month she runs out of money. This past month her water was turned off for a few days. She'd like to take on a part-time second job, but her physical health and emotional exhaustion make that idea a bit precarious. A second job would be good for the budget, but probably not so good for her health.

This has been a depressing and vulnerable scenario. Recently, after we brainstormed about possibilities—look for a new job, get a second job, sell the house, get a roommate, get food stamps, go to the local food bank, anything that popped into our heads—I took an intuitive leap of faith and decided to ask her about her faith. How was it informing her life right now? Where was she seeing God in all of this? How was she praying? She and I kept silent for a minute or so. She looked pensive. Searching. Then she began to share her thoughts. A light came on in her eyes as she told me of a colleague at work who gave her $10 for gas. Another who brought her some vegetables from his garden said, "Just add some meat and you'll have dinner." When she told him she didn't have any meat in the refrigerator, he began to share his meat-filled sandwiches with her. Another friend left food for her dog on her front porch, and a neighbor recently noticed that her taillight was out and offered to fix that for her. A friend she hadn't seen in a while called and wanted to go out for an evening. When she said she couldn't go out because of finances, her friend offered to pay the bill for a casual dinner and an evening of laughter.

"What's different?" I asked.

"I am telling people the truth," she said.

She had decided to swallow her pride and ask for help when she needed it. She wasn't covering up what it was like to live on $1,800 a month. She knew exactly where her money was going and she was willing to tell people. She is an example of the "working poor," and as she got brave enough to tell her story, her friends and colleagues stepped in to help.

There is a great paradox in the Christian faith. We are not Jesus, and we are Jesus. We are not likely to raise people from the dead or turn water into wine. In that way we are not like Jesus. But if we do not know ourselves as Jesus' hands and feet, then we will miss opportunities to enhance and restore the kingdom that is right now. These words below, attributed to Teresa of Avila, are not meant to be metaphor, but a literal, practical, sacred truth:

> Christ has no body but yours,
> no hands but yours,
> no feet but yours.
> Yours are the eyes through which Christ's compassion
> is to look out to the world.
> Yours are the feet with which Christ
> is to go around doing good.
> Yours are the hands with which Christ
> is to bless all people now.

When I take and digest communion, I am incorporating the risen and living Christ into my own body. Therefore, we can lean on each other and not only feel the support of each other, but feel the arms of the risen Christ.

When we see and hear the truth of another, and when we are brave enough to tell our own truth, then we can all be Christ to each other. I know my client will return these favors when she can. The circle keeps giving and is unbroken.

They gave me time, they gave me kindness,
They gave me a room upstairs so that I could lay low.
Funny how I prayed in the darkness to Jesus
And I saw him in these faces that I know.
So I've been leaning on my friends like the arms of Jesus
How they hold me up.

—Tom Conlon

DIGGING DEEPER

1. When was the last time you allowed yourself to lean on some friends? What is that experience like for you?

2. What changes do you experience in your body when you allow yourself to lean on, depend on a friend or family member?

3. Are you better at leaning or being leaned on? Consider this possibility: If we never lean on others, we are cheating them out of a chance to be the body of Christ to us.

4. What resistance do you feel when thinking about yourself as the actual body of Christ? Richard Rohr, Franciscan monk and writer, reminds us that Christ is not Jesus' last name. Christ is the energy that existed with God before the world began. Christ is the Word. We all have the "Word" in us, and want and need opportunities to express that. The Word is in you, too. How do you accept or resist that truth?

5. Dependence, Independence, Interdependence. These are three psycho/spiritual states that we are all supposed to move through. In terms of your friends and family, where do you see yourself? In relationship with the Holy One, where do you see yourself?

Who Is My Neighbor?

Do unto others as you would have others do unto you.
—Matthew 7:12, Luke 6:31

This is the great commandment and the second is like unto it. Love your neighbor as yourself.
—Mark 12:31

Maria, my twenty-six year old daughter, evacuated Manhattan on a Friday evening in September because Hurricane Irene was predicted to clobber the island. Earlier in the day a best friend's mother called her from Cornwall, New York. "Sweetie, this is your Mama Shirley. Now I want you to get on a train and come up here and stay with us. Don't worry about anything. We've got plenty of beds and food." And so she went with two other friends to the loving and caring home of a girlfriend's mom. She received other offers during the day, one from an aunt who lives upstate and another from a family friend in New Jersey. People were definitely watching out for each other.

On Saturday, when I called to see how she was doing, I reminded her to make herself useful. She told me that not only had she and her friends made breakfast, but that they were now also bailing out the basement, which had flooded with water.

Good news, I thought. One favor returned by another. Mama Shirley made sure that she had a warm and welcoming bed. And she offered her hosts her youthful strength that could bail water. When I heard the following morning that a gas main had broken in the middle of the night and they were all evacuated from the house, I had a confidence that everything would be okay. Someone would help. Knowing help would come eased my sense of distance and helplessness.

I watched as this scenario played out up and down the East Coast: friends and families reaching out to others to help get them out of harm's way. I've heard that it was the most orderly and safe mass evacuation in the history of hurricane seasons. Often in these times of trouble and crisis, we experience the generosity of the human spirit. We see people reaching out to help. We see and experience the compassion and goodness in others and in ourselves. We are stretched beyond our comfort zones, outside of our daily lives, and can be reminded of what really matters. Love. Connectedness. Family. Friends. Safety.

As I write this, we are coming up on the tenth anniversary of 9/11. This was another time I watched from hundreds of miles away as friends and family lived through a horrific trauma. It was also a time when I witnessed the amazing capacity of the human spirit. New Yorkers, often misunderstood as rude and uncaring, showed the world the complexity of their spirits, especially the extent of their toughness, the depths of their compassion, and their unflinching devotion to their city. The rest of the world in turn demonstrated that the very fiber of our existence is love and generosity. We saw this, too, with Hurricanes Hugo and Katrina, and most recently with Super Storm Sandy. It wasn't the government that made the difference. It was the people.

I have friends and clients who are involved in other crises around the world. The ongoing crises in Haiti, Somalia, Afghanistan, Pakistan—pick your trouble spot—continue to call for our support and compassion. Remember, too, that there is plenty of need right in our own neighborhoods: a child who doesn't have a decent home or enough food to get through the weekend; a sick or elderly person, shut in, lonely, and in need of a visit; a person without a home, looking for a hot meal and a kind smile: a friend in need of a listening ear and a prayer; an abandoned animal in need of a home.

The golden rule, the second commandment given by Jesus, love your neighbor as yourself, is often, I believe, misunderstood. It's the "as yourself" part that I think we don't hear. Not "as much as yourself." That would make our actions dependent upon our own warped self-images and perverted egos. The commandment is to love my neighbor as if he or she were myself. As *myself*. We are joined. Connected. There is no real separation. Everyone is my neighbor. And I am everyone's neighbor. Anything I do for you or against you, I am ultimately doing to myself.

So here's to Shirley and Eugene, who took my daughter in. I know I would do the same thing for their daughter, and I pray they know that. Here's to all the folks who are reaching out to continue to lend a helping hand, on the East Coast of our country, or anywhere at all in the world. And here's a prayer that we will, all of us, remember that we are all connected, and that what happens to one of us happens to all of us.

DIGGING DEEPER

1. Who is my neighbor? This question has challenged academics and theologians for centuries: Did Jesus mean those close to us geographically? Did he mean friends and family? Did he mean all of humanity? Just whom, exactly, did Jesus mean?

2. Many believe Jesus meant all of humanity. How do you "love" all of humanity as if they were you? What do we do with such an impossible commandment?

3. How has helping out a neighbor been helpful to you? Have you ever been hurt by helping someone out? What was that experience like?

4. We now live in a global world. We can communicate with almost anyone at all in the world. We can send prayers, messages, and money at the touch of a finger. We can receive images and words instantaneously. How has this helped or hindered in your understanding of the second great commandment?

5. How could you allow your daily life to be a part of how you understand this commandment? For example, what would happen if you thought about what you buy at the grocery store as affecting someone in another part of the country or the world? How would you consider the clothes you buy, the water your drink or use, or the car you drive as having an impact on "your neighbor"? It's a lot to think about and overwhelming at times. Start with just one thing.

Worth the Effort

In my community we spend most of our time doing three things: preparing for rituals, participating in rituals, and recovering from rituals.
—Malidoma Somé[38]

I had plans to attend a Bar Mitzvah in New York on Saturday, February 20, 2010. The weather forecast was calling for a blizzard to hit the city on Thursday evening, and I was to leave on Friday. As the forecast continued to worsen on Thursday, I began to worry. "I've got to get there. It's too important to miss," I kept repeating as if that would change things. I barely slept that night. I'm a former Yankee girl. This kind of thing is nothing for New Yorkers. They'll have the airports running in no time and it will all be fine. I hoped if I convinced myself, the weather would be convinced as well.

But my Friday flight was cancelled. Amy, my childhood friend and the mother of Lyle and Evan, the twins to be Bar Mitzvahed, was crying when she answered my phone call. "This is horrible," she said. "I have people flying in from all over the country. I'm worried about *everything*." From years of friendship I knew what everything meant to Amy. It meant everything. She is a perfectionist, a detail-oriented person, an artist. She was worried about e-v-e-ry-thing.

I tried to console her with words that I knew were true, but that sounded so hollow. "You can't do anything about this, Sweetie. It will be what it will be. I'm going to do everything in my power to be there tomorrow. I know everyone will. Hang in there. I love you."

I was able to get myself booked on a flight for the following morning. I used the time that was freed up by the cancellation to do some office work that was in a pile on the side of my desk. Bills, correspondence, insurance problems. "There. Something good accomplished from something so disappointing." It felt good to finish off a pile of work.

As I thought through what the next morning might hold, I called my daughter and asked if she could change her plans. Instead of taking a bus to the airport to meet me and then picking up a rental car, could she meet me at the airport with the rental car in her possession so that we could lose no time and race from the airport to the temple. I went to bed that night with an earnest but ridiculously childish prayer. "Please God, if there's any way for me to get there, I'd be grateful."

I was at the airport at 5:30 a.m. ready for a Bar Mitzvah. Dressed in black velvet and bejeweled appropriately, make-up on, and tingling with anticipation, I walked confidently through the terminal and went through security. Many people stared, especially those who had slept on the floor of the airport the night before. With rumpled clothes, matted hair, and frustrated expressions, they looked patronizingly at me as if I was cute and naïve. When I got to the gate, a man who was still lying across a few seats looked at me and cocked his head. "Hey Lady, don't you know there was a blizzard up there?" I pointed to the plane waiting outside the window and the red gate sign that said "CLT-EWR 7:00 AM ON-TIME."

"Looks like we're going on time," I replied. Could it possibly be?

As the plane began its bumpy ascent, an older gentleman next to me commented on how much he hated turbulence, which began our conversation. I considered it a good omen that he was the rabbi of a congregation in Charlotte. He was thrilled and touched that I was flying up to attend a Bar Mitzvah. "It's sure to be worth the effort," he said with a smile. "Absolutely." I responded.

The plane landed at 9:15 a.m. and we walked into the temple at 10:15, only fifteen minutes late. A few other latecomers, men, grabbed yarmulkes as the ushers greeted us all with huge smiles and said, "We're so glad you made it. We've been on the lookout for you." The sanctuary was full, but we found a few empty chairs in the back. We grabbed the prayer books, thinking we would follow along, and then stifled laughs as we opened them. The books were in Hebrew and read right to left, back to front. We put the prayer books back down and listened to the cantor who was singing something hauntingly beautiful. A few deep breaths later, we had settled into the ritual.

As I looked around and continued to listen, I was struck by the importance of this sacred event. The family members were all sitting together in the front. The boys, their father, and grandfathers looked so handsome in their suits and tallises. The Torah was paraded around the sanctuary to a familiar tune known as "The Torah Song." Finally, something we were able to sing! It allowed us to join in the jubilation. The sacred text was wrapped in a mantle that Amy had designed and made as a gift to the temple. Intricate beading and embroidery depicting the tree of life, pomegranates, and leaves of all kind covered the mantle. People reached out to touch it as it passed by. We touched it too, the rabbi smiling generously as he passed our seats.

The boys' parents each gave an intimate speech emphasizing the importance of their children's devotion and hard work in their three years of Hebrew school, the importance of the support of family and friends, and the gratitude they owed to the rabbi and the cantor, the men who had personally invested in their children and had made their Jewish faith alive and meaningful to them.

The rabbi spoke directly to the boys. He spoke of their intelligence, their sense of humor, their unique gifts, and their relationship as twins. He encouraged them never to stop laughing, to enjoy their faith and the good life that God has given them. The boys read and chanted from the Torah, accomplished and mature. They each gave a talk about something important in their lives. Evan spoke of his love for animals and his desire to be a part of saving endangered animals from extinction. Lyle spoke of ending prejudice, and of treating all people with compassion and kindness.

Grandparents, too, read from the Torah. The service concluded with the presentation of a loaf of challah bread as big as a football, a large chalice of wine, and an invitation to come to the front of the synagogue to eat and drink, which we did.

At the reception I was reunited with some high school friends and met their spouses and children. All but two of the 200 people invited had braved the blizzard and been able to get there. Watching as the teenagers played games led by an energetic and loud DJ and then danced in that self-conscious middle-school way, I remembered my own child as a teenager, becoming a young woman.

I clapped and circled in a whirling frenzy as Amy and her husband, Peter, were lifted high in the air in chairs, "Hava Nagila" playing raucously in the background. I danced with friends, strangers, and acquaintances. I ate a four-course meal and drank good wine. When it was over, all of us were happy and exhausted. I had worn myself out helping them celebrate.

This is how it ought to be with these powerful rituals of our faith and community. We come together to celebrate landmarks and to witness to God's forming of us. If we are the hosts, we gather those who love and support us, asking once again for their love and support. We give thanks for all that is good, for the abundance God places in our lives, and we share abundantly of those gifts. If we are the guests, we remember that we live in community, that we offer our love and presence to another, and that attending these rituals changes us as much as it marks a change in the participants. What we do in community matters. For the host and guest alike, it is worth making the effort, spending the money, spending the time, spending ourselves for them.

DIGGING DEEPER

1. What rituals in your life have been particularly important to you? How much effort was required for these rituals to occur?

2. What is the largest amount of money you have spent for a ritual? What principle underlies the decision to spend money like that? Have you ever spent yourself, pouring all of your energy and resources into the preparation and celebration of a ritual? What was the experience like?

3. What is the difference between being a spectator at a ritual and being a participant? Have you done both? What was the experience like?

4. What traditions or rituals are a part of your faith community? How are they meaningful to you? Have any of them lost their meaning? If so, how would you explain this?

5. What rituals would you like to see included in your faith community? Where are the gaps?

6. How have rituals transformed you?

The Creative Reality of Relationships

Owning our stories and loving ourselves through that process is the bravest thing that we will ever do.
—Brené Brown[39]

"Tell me about this family."

This is often the opening line in a family therapy session. I learned it from the masters in the field. "Tell me about this family."

What usually follows is someone starts talking about someone else, usually the person creating what looks like trouble in the family. Or maybe someone starts talking about personal problems. "He is always creating trouble. Every weekend we wonder if he will come home before curfew." Or, "She is just a pain in the neck. She can't leave anything alone and she's a control freak."

When I interrupt and say, "No, tell me about this *family*," there is often silence.

The family is an entity of its own. It is a creation, a creative endeavor. What does this family feel like? Look like? What are its characteristics? When does it smell sweet? Rotten? What pieces fit? What doesn't work? If you could sculpt it, paint it, or dance it, what would it look like? Who protects this creation? What are the values and principles that guide the creative process of this family?

I ask the same question about marriages.

"Tell me about this marriage."

Again, this directive often stumps the couple in my office.

"I thought I was just going to be able to complain about him," one thinks secretly. "Can't you just fix her?"

Like a family, a marriage is its own creation. It can be damaged, sometimes beyond repair. Once, during a session in my office, I compared the marriage of the couple to a thick marine rope. Every time one of the partners hurled insults, a little razor blade cut a few threads of the rope. Without repair, the rope became even more weakened. The next series of insults, dismissals, disrespect, secrets, or betrayals, and the rope is cut again, each successive tear compromising the strength of the marriage. Eventually, the rope is beyond repair. Now your rope is severed. You have no rope (marriage) and you have to decide if you want to start over again with a new one. If we could think about our families and marriages in this way, as creative works, I think we would handle them with more care. What would happen if, when we walked down the street together or through a store together, our marriage creation or our family creation could be seen, like a work of art? When we are connected and caring, perhaps a bright light would surround us and move energetically between us. Not only would *we* notice it, but the light would shine to those around us. If we knew that as we spent a morning blaming and shaming each other, a dark black cloud would hover over us and around those we love, would that change our actions and awareness? I believe we would be more thoughtful, creative, sacrificial, and sacramental about our relationships if we thought about what we were creating. If we thought of them as works of art.

Friendships, too, are an entity, a creation. Not just two people but the "creation" that is the friendship. And communities have their own energy, their own feel. If you could see your community as a sculpture, painting, or dance, what would that image look like? What is your contribution to the creation?

The field of marriage and family therapy has evolved from the early years of experimenting with techniques, to the present time when research and data help us understand what works and what doesn't. We know what is most damaging and likely to kill a marriage, as well as what is most helpful and likely to bring life to it. My colleagues who travel the world helping families and couples tell me that the presenting problems are the same wherever they go: not being understood and accepted, shame, power, and betrayals of trust. Underneath the presentation, the real problem is this: people forget that the relationship is its own thing, its own entity, its own ongoing creation. It must be tended to, worked on, looked at, and revised. Sometimes the initial contract, spoken or unspoken, has to be ditched and a new one agreed upon. And always, yes always, more than one person has wrought the creation or destruction. So each of us must look at how we are contributing to this creation. We have to do the deep and often hard work of looking at ourselves. There is no way around that truth.

The good news is that it is often in these intimate relationships, with the ones that we are closest to, that the most potential for transformation exists.

DIGGING DEEPER

1. If you could sculpt the family in which you grew up, what would it look like? What colors, textures, shapes, and images would this sculpture contain? If you are inclined, try sculpting or drawing this image. Share it with another person or in a group setting.

2. Do the same with the closest relationships you currently have. A marriage or life partnership. A relationship with a child or children. What images and colors come to you as you create a representation of each of these relationships?

3. How do you think you would act differently if you could see your own effect on a relationship? For example, if you were watching a piece of art being created by the way you parent a child day by day, how do you think it would affect your parenting?

4. There are many studies available now that show how prayer can influence people and circumstances, even if the people do not know they are being held in prayer. If you pray for a relationship or for a friend, what do you think your prayer is doing for that relationship or person? In other words, how would you explain why you pray for someone?

5. Other studies show that telling your story or your truth to another person and having it heard actually changes your brain chemistry. What implications does this research have for your relationships with others?

The Love that Lies Beneath
the Woe

The unconscious rules the world.
—Carl Whitaker[40]

Once, when I was a novice therapist, I was privileged to watch an internationally renowned master therapist work with a struggling family. The family had come, they said, because of a fourteen-year-old girl, whose mother was only seventeen years old when she was born. The girl was acting out, skipping school, defying curfew, and sneaking out her bedroom window to meet her boyfriend. Pulling a chair away from the others and slumping into it, the girl pulled her knees up high in front of her chest. The mom and her husband sat in two other chairs, each holding a younger child on their lap. Mom's parents were there, too, looking very proper and nervous, hands folded, ankles crossed.

About fifteen minutes into the session, the therapist had everyone in the family take off their shoes and put them in a pile in the middle of the room; then he added his own.

"This is the pile of family shit. Somehow this has to be sorted out. During this session, you can only speak if you take one of your shoes off the pile and talk about how you are now or have been contributing to this pile of junk. My shoes are in this pile because you have invited me to be a part of your family system for a little while, and I know I bring my own issues and projections with me."

A long period of silence ensued. The father/stepfather was the first to take one of his black wing-tips off the pile. He spoke of how judgmental he had been by refusing to accept his step-daughter for who she was, and for not realizing how hard it would be to raise a child that was not his own. He spoke of feelings of resentment.

When he stopped talking, there was a long silence. Minutes seemed like hours. Who would pick up a shoe next? Finally, the maternal grandmother reached for her plain brown loafer. When she spoke, she recounted how rigid she had been as a young mother, calling her daughter derogatory names when she started dating, taking out all of her own fear of sexual promiscuity on her daughter. At this very moment, a family secret came out. She stunned everyone when she said, "I got pregnant in high school. I was sent away to a home and had my baby there. I never saw the child who was given up for adoption." She was telling this secret now, she said, because of her deep love for her granddaughter and her desire that she wouldn't be troubled or sick.

Sobs. Silence. Shame.

Understanding. Light. Freedom.

The session went on in this vein for over an hour, people talking about their responsibility in this thing we call family. The room became a safe space for the people to talk about their fears, shames, joys, sorrows, and dreams.

There is always plenty of blame to go around. Things don't get messy overnight. The pile of shit builds over generations of people and circumstances. And sometimes, usually during another crisis, there may be the opportunity to slow down and take a look at how each of us and all of us contribute to the pile. There is no way to go forward in health without all parties taking responsibility for their contribution to the pile. No family is spared. Perhaps some families have more shit than others, but trouble, drama, and struggle are the way of life, as old as human history.

I am reminded of a sermon written by the Reverend Doctor Mark Jones which recounts the Old Testament story in Genesis

37, of Joseph and his brothers betraying each other and making power plays, repeating and reinforcing the same problems they had been dealing with for years. As Jones unravels the story, he explores how family wounds are acted out. At the end of the sermon he says,

> Being honest about the family's wounds is no easy matter. It wasn't easy for Joseph and his brothers. It's not easy for us. Some of the past is not easy to forgive. Some of it is not easy to love. But understand, we're not called to be any more perfect than this tragically flawed family whose story is somehow like our own. And as Carlyle Marney once said, "We do not let our failure to love perfectly keep us from loving as best we can. To be responsible means to face all that makes us shamed and uncomfortable, and to continue to press for the love that lies beneath the woe."[41]

This is my prayer for families, communities, states, nations, and the world. That we can, each of us, and all of us, face all that makes us shamed and uncomfortable. That we will make changes to ourselves and our families that will help us go forward with more health and more consciousness, and, in doing so, we will continue to press for the love that lies beneath the woe.

DIGGING DEEPER

1. Consider a recent problem in your family. Spend some time thinking, as honestly as possible, about your contribution to that problem. How would you describe it? How would you be able and willing to articulate your contribution to the problem to others involved?

2. What do we mean by sayings such as "blood is thicker than water"? What do you think keeps people hanging in there even when the going gets tough? What do you think allows people to leave when the going gets tough?

3. How is it possible for one person to change a system? If you have had this experience, write about it or talk about it in a group.

4. Whether we experience another positively or negatively is not always a conscious act. There are many factors that make up how we interact with people. Have you ever had a very positive or very negative reaction to someone without understanding exactly why? Share this with another or in a group and talk about what that was like for you.

5. Consider the quotation at the beginning of this essay, "The unconscious rules the world." Talk about it with a friend or in a group.

V.

VOCATION:

WHAT'S CALLING YOU NOW?
LIVING THE TRANSFORMATION

Whether or not a man arrives or does not arrive at his own destiny—the place that is peculiarly his—depends on whether or not he finds the Kingdom within and hears the call to wholeness—or holiness, as another might say. The man who hears that call is chosen. He does not have to scramble for a place in the scheme of things. He knows that there is a place that is his and that he can live close to the One who will show it to him. Life becomes his vocation.

—Elizabeth O'Connor[42]

The third of four children and a whopping 9 pounds, 8 ounces, my mother was grateful that I slept through the night almost immediately. She described me as easy, level, and adaptable. Yet, when the environment was in turmoil or something difficult was going on, like marital arguments, sibling fights, or extended family issues, I was hyper-alert, anxious, and observant. I developed a paradoxical temperament.

Specifically, there was much death going on in my extended family from the time my mother and father conceived me until the time I was six years old. Mom used to say, "People were dying left and right." I was "nursed on grief," my mother told me several times when I was old enough to understand. That wasn't a metaphorical statement. My mother breastfed me, and for that reason, I was taken to many of the family funerals and was nursed right there at the funeral home or at the funeral itself. I think this is why I have always loved the phrase from Isaiah 53:3 "acquainted with grief," and I believe this preverbal acquaintance partially formed my way of being in the world.

The word *vocation* has as its root the Latin word *vocare*, which means to *call forth* or to *call out of*. When our true temperament is "called forth," our most natural way of *being* in the world is allowed and received. In their book, *Healing the Purpose of Your Life*, Dennis, Sheila, and Matthew Linn call our special way of being in the world our "sealed orders." This doesn't have to do with a particular job or career path. Our personal vocation has to do with how we *are* in the world in our most natural and loving/loved state. How do we give love? How do we receive love? When are we most truly content?

In my most natural state, I am a caregiver. I create spaces where people can rest, grieve, be nourished, learn, and heal. Sometimes I use the words "hearth maker" because I like to create a sense of belonging and community wherever I go. That is my personal vocation.

We often find our professional vocations when we are living and loving out of our personal vocation. My personal vocation of "hearth maker" took me first into the field of education. I loved teaching in all its forms. I taught gymnastics as a teenager, and I was sought after as a coach because I created a sense of community and belonging for the children. While I was in college I started a dance program in the Greenville, South Carolina "mini-parks"—parks in underserved neighborhoods where dance lessons for children were the last thing on anybody's mind. All the neighborhood children were welcome and there was a great sense of *esprit de corps* and community. Later, as a middle-school teacher, my classroom was the hangout place. I wanted the kids to feel like they were welcome in my room. With my wonderful team teacher, Susan Wolfe, we created a team approach, mixing and melding different disciplines so that the curriculum was taught as a whole. If Susan was teaching the geography of the Southwest in Social Studies, I taught the students about Southwestern literature and art. If I was teaching proper nutrition in health, Susan would teach math by asking the kids to add calories or to multiply what one daily order of French fries over the course of a year added up to. We worked together, and we even gave our team a name, The M&W Sensations. Recently I bumped into a former student at a music event. She introduced me to her thirteen-year-old daughter saying, "This was my sixth-grade teacher. I was an M&W Sensation." Almost thirty years later, she remembered the community we created together.

As my vocational path took me into the field of psychotherapy, my personal vocation, that of hearth maker, continued. I was determined to gather around me a group of thoughtful, collaborative, spiritual, and competent therapists and create a sense of community among us. It is important to me that my office feel like a warm and welcoming place, like a home. From the welcome at the front door—meditative music in the waiting room, fresh coffee and water, soothing colors and art designed to evoke feelings of acceptance and welcome—I want people to feel nurtured and nourished. This doesn't negate the difficult work that gets done or the hard things that get said during the therapy relationship, but the sense of hospitality and hearth flow beneath and give foundation to the often-difficult work of healing and transformation. A mentor of mine says that the relationship is the anesthesia for the psychic surgery that must take place.

By writing about my personal vocational journey, I hope to give you one way to think about vocation. So many people I know wrestle with this topic, and I believe it is because they start from the wrong end of the equation. Step one of the journey is to know your unique way of being in the world. Knowing what brings you joy, freedom, contentment, and a sense of unity. Once you can identify these things, it matters less what you are *doing* as long as you can *be* yourself at least most of the time. So, I can teach, counsel, cook, consult, write, coach, entertain, decorate, dance, or garden, and the theme of the river that flows underneath all the *doing* is the essence of my *being*, which is caregiving, hearth making, and hospitality.

There is a phrase in the hymn "Take My Life and Let It Be" (*The Hymnal 1982*, Hymn 707) that captures the essence of personal vocation. In the first verse the author uses the language of moving "at the impulse of [God's] love." To me, that is the language of personal vocation. When we allow our hands, our intellect, and our wills to *be* the unique way that God created them to be, then we will live with our whole selves in our own unique vocation. And when we live that way, in whatever activity we find ourselves, our lives will touch others and the world will be changed.

This is the last section of this book on transformation, last because I believe that when we live out of that transformed place, we live out of the place of our calling, out of that place of having our authentic voice. Some of the essays in this section depict people who appear to be living out their calling. They have stepped into the flow of their authentic selves and are sharing that clearly in the world. Sometimes, however, deciphering our vocations can be difficult and tedious. Doing the deep inner work, paying attention to the gifts of Holy Ground that we are offered, making space to allow the Holy Other to speak to us, and living in community are all tools to help us engage life from a vocational perspective.

As you are reading this section, think about your own special way of being in the world. What brings you pleasure? How do you like to show your love? How do you like to be loved? What swells your heart with gratitude? What are you doing when you lose track of time? Once you allow yourself to luxuriate in your vocational qualities, whatever work you are doing will have a greater sense of wholeness and holiness. I truly believe that when we live out of our truest selves, out of our personal vocation, not only are we transformed, but also we transform the world.

Be Careful What You Pray For

Your children are not your children. They are the sons and daughters of
Life's longing for itself.
They come through you but not from you,
And though they are with you yet they belong not to you.
—Kahlil Gibran[43]

I have several favorite prayers in The Book of Common Prayer. A particular favorite is said during the service of Holy Baptism, and ends with these words:

> Sustain them, O Lord, in your Holy Spirit. Give them an inquiring and discerning heart, the courage to will and to persevere, a spirit to know and to love you, and the gift of joy and wonder in all your works. Amen.

On a recent Sunday, after watching eight soft, pink, noisy babies, and one very happy adult receive the sacrament of baptism, we prayed this prayer, and I thought, "Could we wish anything more radical and meaningful for our children? Do we really mean these words?"

"Give her an inquiring and discerning mind." If she (or he) really got this kind of mind, she might disagree with me. She might have her own thoughts and reach her own conclusions, and they might be very different from my own. She might end up believing things about God that I don't believe. She might be more conservative (or liberal, or free, or tolerant, or prejudiced) than I am. She might take me to task on my own thoughts, my blind spots, my orthodoxies, and my own unconscious process, and that might not feel very good. In short, she might be my Zen Master. Do I really want to pray for this?

"Give him the courage to will and to persevere." But only, Lord, if he's not using that strong will and perseverance to push back against me. We don't like "strong-willed children." There are books published about how to deal with these challenging, high-spirited little ones. And yet, here we are, praying for that specifically. And then, Sweet Jesus, if he really gets to know and love you, he might just want to turn life upside down, just like you did. He might not be orderly and diplomatic. He might not be socially or politically correct. He might even be outspoken at church.

At the end there's the part about the "gift of wonder in all your works." Children naturally have the gift of wonder, if we don't scare it out of them. Maybe we're really praying that for ourselves, so we don't dry up and miss what is right before our eyes. Do I still have the gift of wonder? Can I wonder as much about myself as I do about others? I did enjoy wondering about and talking to the bird that seemed to be calling to me this morning as I sat on the front porch, tying my sneakers for my early morning walk.

"It's a beeeautiful day, Miss Amy, don't you agree? Sparkling. Magnificent. Don't miss it."

"Thanks for reminding me, Mr. Bird. But it is only 6:30, you know. Some people are still trying to sleep."

"I'm a bird, Miss Amy. This is what I do. I get up early and I sing my heart out. I can't imagine anyone would take exception to this. You've got to be who you are, you know."

"You're right, Mr. Bird. I've got to be who I am."

So here's my prayer for the newly baptized. Be yourself. Listen for, find, and nurture the calling that is yours. Grow into the unique God-seed that you are. Never stop being amazed and wondering at the world. And if all of that is a little tough on your parents and those around you, be patient with them. They just need to be reminded of what they prayed for.

DIGGING DEEPER

1. What does it mean to you to have an inquiring and discerning heart?

2. On a scale of one to ten, how courageous are you? What holds you back? What pushes you forward?

3. How do you take joy and pleasure in nature? How would you describe your relationship to the natural world?

4. Who has most encouraged you to be yourself? How did they offer that encouragement? What do you think they saw in you?

5. Who is a person in your life, adult or child, whose gifts and calling you can clearly see? How do you encourage this person?

6. What do you need more of or less of in your daily life in order for you to live into your vocation?

Diving In

You will not fully discover your gifts until you are first willing to fear-lessly share them with the world.
—Dennis Merritt Jones[44]

The sky looked threatening, black clouds building up in the dis-tance as we headed out on Lake Murray. Our original plan was to anchor the boat and swim for a while, so we knew that if we wanted to get in a swim, we'd better do it immediately. No thun-der yet, but certainly the possibility was looming.

I was the first one in, excited and ready to feel the cool lake water against my skin and wanting as much time in the lake as possible before the weather forced us out. I was wiping my eyes, waiting for my contacts to re-focus, and reaching for a Styrofoam noodle that someone had thrown my way when I heard these words: "I don't swim."

Turning my head, I saw Bob in the water close to the boat, a noodle under his arm, splashing around a bit trying to stay bal-anced. Another friend, still on board said, "Well then, let's throw you another noodle," and he gave Bob a second noodle. This helped to keep his head well above water.

"Did I just hear you say 'I don't swim'?" I gurgled in disbelief, spitting lake water out as I jostled the noodle under my own arm.

"Yes. I never learned to swim as a child and when I've tried as an adult, I just sink."

"You just jumped off a boat into a lake and you don't swim? Are you serious?" I asked again.

And then we all burst into an odd mix of laughter and under-the-breath comments. Did he just do what I think he did? What the hell was he thinking? Was he drinking? There was, of course, the immediate relief that he was safe and laughing with us. Then there was the sibling-like teasing, rightfully earned: *Glad you told us* before *you jumped in. Way to go, Friend. Good thing we had an extra noodle. Is anyone here a lifeguard?* His wife of forty-two years wasn't exactly laughing, more just offering her position: "I've stopped trying to save him," she said, floating on her back and paddling away, annoyed.

I couldn't stop thinking about this as the night wore on. This man, my friend Bob, just dove into a lake knowing he couldn't swim. And then I thought, in so many ways, that is a metaphor for his life. He grew up in an impoverished home, his mother not knowing how to read or write. He learned as much as he could in public school, and then headed off to college without any guidance from home and not having any idea what awaited him there. After college, he *dove in* to seminary, and as his life in the ministry progressed, he *dove in* to job after job, new ministry after new ministry, figuring it out as he went along. He's usually up for a challenge and seems to have an open mind when it comes to new experiences. He is unpretentious and doesn't call much attention to himself. He is not "high maintenance."

He is, though, a little like the disciples. They sure didn't know what they were getting into. Mostly it was on-the-job training, figuring things out as they went along. None of them was particularly suited for the position, and they all had to dive in and figure things out. They didn't worry about having the most up-to-date skills, speaking the common language, or having enough money. They did seem to rely on each other periodically for community and assurance. Other than that, they did what they felt called to do, and God blessed the rest.

Thanks to my friend for sharing this lesson and being a reminder. Sometimes I need to let myself dive in without the security of knowing I can keep myself afloat. I can allow others to throw me a noodle now and then to help me. I do think I'd warn them, though, if I thought their help might save my life.

DIGGING DEEPER

1. What's a good metaphor for your own vocational life? In the case of my friend Bob, "diving in" seemed exactly appropriate. What's an appropriate metaphor for your approach to life?

2. When has a lack of competence or fear of failure affected your decisions and activities?

3. It certainly doesn't appear that Jesus chose the "best and the brightest" to be his disciples. Pick a disciple with whom you are familiar. What do you think Jesus saw in him? What do you think Jesus called out of him? For example, Peter was impulsive and passionate, but Jesus also saw leadership qualities in him.

4. How do you discern when it is important to do your homework and be prepared, and when it is better to be spontaneous and wing it?

5. Reread the quotation at the beginning of this essay. Are you fearlessly able to share your gifts with the world? How?

Samia's Kitchen

That place God calls you is where your heart's deep gladness and the world's deep hunger meet.
—Frederick Buechner[45]

When I moved across town, I found myself in need of a new person to do clothing alterations for me. At a friend's recommendation, I went to the home of Samia, a delightful Lebanese woman. When I stepped over the threshold and into her hallway, the smell of something recently baked filled me.

"It smells great in here," I said, breathing in deeply. "I feel better just smelling it."

"I just made baklava," she replied. "I'll give you a piece on the way out."

After fitting my pants on me, she showed me pictures of her children, her grandchildren, and her late husband. Then she ushered me into her modest kitchen.

"Just one," I said, as she opened the canister to offer me the sweet. She wrapped it carefully in plastic and sent me out the door with a big smile and a tasty treat. I had one bite immediately in the car. Shutting my eyes as the honey and butter dissolved on my tongue, I realized I had a quick decision to make. Get out of the car, knock on the door, tell her I was an idiot to ask for only one and beg for another. Or, make the treat last. I had just met Samia. I wasn't ready yet to embarrass myself and give in to my culinary cravings. So, I decided right then to eat it just one bite at a time. My second bite was after dinner that night, and the last with my morning coffee.

Every time I sat down for another bite, I thought of how my maternal grandmother's house always smelled of something just out of the oven. It is a smell I associate with comfort, love, and plump German women. I don't bake much and I don't eat many sweets. This was a wonderful treat.

When I went back a week later to pick up my altered pants, the house once again smelled of something earthy and delicious, but I couldn't tell what it was. After I tried on my clothing to make sure of the fit, Samia once again led me to her kitchen and held out a stainless steel platter. It was full of small bundles of food that resembled large meatballs. I had no idea what they were. "Kibbeh," she said. "It is my grandson's favorite food. He got an award at high school yesterday, so I am making him his favorite dinner. I am so proud of him," she smiled. She started to eat one right there and encouraged me to do the same. The egg-sized bundle of ground beef, bulgur, pine nuts, and a wonderful blend of nutmeg, cumin, cinnamon, and allspice was too big for me, and my first bite sent bits and crumbles onto the floor. The flavors were comforting, and I *oooed* and *aahhed* as I often do when appreciating delicious food. I am an enthusiastic eater.

"I sure hope your family appreciates you, Samia."

Her answer caught me up short.

"I don't even care. I just cook and feed people because I want to." Her face glowed with pleasure.

Wow. Wanting to be appreciated was *my* issue, not hers. Wanting to hear words of affirmation was my need, not hers. Samia was way ahead of me on this one, just offering her family the things that she could offer, the things that made her happy to offer. She was working from the heart, from the place of personal vocation, of knowing the essence of who she is. It was a selfless offering. She was giving of herself in a way that not only nourished others but nourished her as well.

Frederick Buechner, that great Presbyterian theologian and writer, says that vocation is that place where the world's deep hunger and our deep gladness meet. Perhaps this is Samia's vocation, showing strangers and family hospitality, nourishing their spirits and bodies. Perhaps because she was offering up the desire of her heart, the seed, which God put in her at the making, she was at a place of total peace and balance.

I still hope Samia's family appreciates her. If it doesn't matter to her, it might matter to them. Having a grateful heart and an expressive mind is never a bad thing. So thank you, Samia, not only for the homemade Lebanese food, but also for the chance to learn, again, that when we live from our own uniqueness, not much else matters.

DIGGING DEEPER

∞

1. Who do you know who, like Samia, seems absolutely content in doing what s/he does? What do you think it is that creates their sense of contentment?

2. When you are offering your gifts to the world, what gives you affirmation or encouragement? Can you explain what that is like for you? If you feel like you are not receiving affirmation for your gifts, what changes would you be willing to make to live and work in a way so that you are affirmed?

3. When are you most content? When does time seem to fly for you?

4. If you had a day that was the perfect vocational day, what would you be doing?

5. In some very simple ways, Samia changed my world. What are some simple ways that others have changed your world?

The Chaplain's Prayer

Last
Night
God
Posted
On the Tavern wall
A hard decree for Love's inmates
Which read:
If your heart cannot find joyful work
The jaws of this world
Will probably
Grab hold of your
Sweet
Ass.
—Hafiz[46]

We were asked to stand for the invocation. The chaplain of the new Charleston County Detention Center, Eva Smith, was wearing her dress-blue uniform, cuffs adorned in gold brocade. She looked out at us and said, "We're getting ready to pray to God Almighty and to thank him for the miracle that we have all been a part of, and I'd like to start with a hand-clapping."

The two hundred or so people who were gathered for this ribbon-cutting ceremony put their hands together for a lukewarm hand-clapping. The chaplain began praying and after a few sentences, stopped and waited. There was a long silence.

"Can I have an 'Amen'?"

"Amen," came a strong voice from the row behind me. A meeker response came from the back of the crowd.

"God, we are thankful for the vision it took to build this jail. For the vision of the county council and the tireless work of those members who insisted on a decent facility. And not only did we get a decent facility, we got a state-of-the-art facility. We are so thankful, God."

"Amen. Amen. Yes, Lord, we are thankful," came the roll of voices from the crowd.

And away we went. For five minutes she prayed for many important things. She prayed for the inmates, for the state of their hearts. She prayed for their families. She prayed for the detention staff who would be working with them, for law enforcement, for the kitchen workers, the doctors and nurses, and the laundry workers. She thanked God for the architects and construction workers who had made this building a reality, and expressed thanks for the innovative design that offered the best hope of rehabilitation. During and especially after each petition, a wave of "Amen" rolled through the room, affirming the thanksgiving. When she was finished praying, she asked us for another hand-clapping, and then turned the program over to the sheriff. The architect sitting next to my husband leaned over to me and said, "I really need to learn how to pray."

I didn't have time to ask what struck him about the prayer, but my suspicion was that it was the unapologetic authority and competence the chaplain brought to this invocation. Usually at events like this, affairs that are filled with dignitaries, politicians, and managers of every kind, the invocation, if there is one, is benign, stale, and rudimentary. It's almost like a required statement that says we believe in a Higher Power and it is the right, politically correct thing to do to mention that.

But this chaplain took her job seriously. She prayed with true devotion and passion. She did that in the manner and style that came from her evangelical faith tradition. No written notes. No attempts to be politically correct. No worries that all the people running for elected office were there. She was confident in her role: chaplain of this detention center. And she was confident in her own style of praying. It mattered. I felt it in the room. People's minds were quieted and their attention was on giving thanks. They were paying attention to the important matters at hand, and for just a moment the pomp and circumstance of this political occasion was put aside, and God and our hearts were center stage.

After she finished and we sat back down, she took a moment to thank her volunteer chaplains, who, she said, spent countless hours with inmates—befriending them, praying with them, reading the Bible with them, listening to them, mirroring the love and redemptive powers of God to them. "I have over forty volunteer chaplains serving with me at this facility. Will those who are here please stand?"

At least thirty men and women stood. It was hard for me to believe that this one facility had so many volunteer chaplains. Yet, after listening to Chaplain Smith pray, I wasn't at all surprised. She was dedicated to her work. Her heart was in it. I imagine that her passion and compassion are contagious. Just by looking, it was clear that ministers from many walks of life and many faith traditions volunteered here. Some wore clerical collars and some wore traditional African headdresses. There were a few in long robes and a couple in fancy suits. Yes, I thought, her integrity is contagious. You'd want to work alongside her.

The architect was right. We all need to learn how to pray. We need to be confident enough in our own faith and in our own way of being that we can pray from the bottom of our hearts, no matter who on earth may be listening. It is our integrity, honesty, and devotion that stir God's heart and our own hearts, not some rote, formulaic words that we speak without thinking about the possibility that prayer can transform us. The desires of our hearts, our true thankfulness, and our deep faith in the work that God is doing in our lives and in the world, are what make a prayer worth praying.

Can I have an *Amen*?

DIGGING DEEPER

1. How would you define prayer? When do you consider your-self praying?

2. How do you pray? Are you more comfortable with spontaneous prayer or written prayer? Why do you think some people prefer written prayers?

3. How do you feel about praying publicly? About being "put on the spot" to pray? Why do you think people have such strong reactions to public prayer?

4. When has another person's unique sense of self felt contagious to you, as if you just want to spend more time around them? What do you think you were experiencing? What was that person calling out of you?

5. How is prayer a part of your vocational life?

For All the Musicians, with Love

For heights and depths no words can reach, music is the soul's own speech.
—Anita Robertson[47]

I couldn't take my eyes off of them. When I tried to shut my eyes to listen more closely to the music, I quickly opened them again because I wanted to see these talented and passionate musicians as they were playing. All five of them, all men dressed in coats and ties, seemed to be in the zone, channeling something that flowed through them along with the blood in their veins. They often closed *their* eyes, but I couldn't take my eyes off of them.

The group was named after Alan Vaché, the jazz clarinetist. A middle-aged, chubby man sporting a Homer Simpson tie, he made his clarinet sound like honey, or maybe taffy . . . stretching and slipping and coming back together to create the sounds that permeated my skin. I've never heard a clarinet sound like this. In between songs he would tell stories about life as a jazz musician. He had a whimsical sense of humor and a dry wit.

I don't remember all of their full names, but the other men in the band were equally impressive. Mark was on piano, fingers sailing across the keys like a prize racing boat. His body rarely moved, but looking at him with his eyes closed and his forehead wrinkling ever so slightly, chin stretching up as if to grab the heavens, I could almost feel his passion for the music. David was on double bass. How is it possible for that mammoth instrument to be graceful? David navigated that instrument with the grace of a ballet dancer . . . up and down and under and over . . . all the while grinning and obviously enjoying himself. I couldn't see John, the drummer, as well as I could the others, but my husband said that he had never heard a set of drums sing. John's drums sang, beautiful sweet music.

For me, the treat of the night was the vibraphonist, Matthew Hammond. Matthew is twenty years old, a handsome blonde man with a baby face. During his solo, "he" almost seemed to disappear as something bigger than "he" took over. He was free, uninhibited, natural, and completely focused. He almost always looked a little shocked when he finished a solo and the audience burst into applause, as if the applause broke the deep trance he was graced with while playing. And then he would smile a smile that lit up the room and I couldn't help but feel that this was a young man who was living into being exactly the person God created him to be.

Most musicians don't have easy lives. Much of the world doesn't value the gifts that they bring to us. They give us a language for our souls, they help us get out of our own way and open our hearts to the heavens, they help us play and relax. In this way they make the world a better place. They remind us that hard work, discipline, and dedication are needed to develop gifts. They remind us that people we might label as "weird" or "nerdy" or "eccentric" or "introverted" are used by God in the most remarkable ways. And yet we continue to cut the arts from our school programs, from our government budgets, and even from our church services, denying some the possibility of discovering their true vocation.

While watching the movie *Titanic* many Christmases ago, I remember how touched I was that the musicians stayed on the deck of the sinking ship, offering their music as a prayer for all the passengers. In the midst of chaos, the musicians remained faithful, selflessly giving of the gift that was uniquely theirs.

After the Twin Towers toppled, musicians came together and held two concerts: "The Concert for New York City" and "America: A Tribute to Heroes." Both of these events were designed to help the people of our country find some meaning in this tragedy. They helped us grieve. They helped us pray. They helped us rally and find courage. They gave us faith in the human spirit. When a loved one gets married or dies, we always want the music to be right. We know on some intuitive level that the music can make or break a ritual.

In this moment, I can only thank the musicians who are willing to risk being who God created them to be. Most of them won't make much money, maybe not even enough to pay the bills. Most of them won't be famous, household names. They will have to work late nights and weekends, and will have to give up many other pleasures to put in the necessary practice time. Many of them will at least occasionally have to live on the road, traveling without family or friends. Somehow, because they can't *not* do what they do, they are okay with all of this. They don't complain, because they are doing what they love. We should take the time to thank them and to allow ourselves to be moved by the gifts they offer us. We can open ourselves to the passion they exhibit and pray that we show forth the same kind of passion in the vocations of *our* lives.

DIGGING DEEPER

1. In the moment, how have you experienced "Holy Ground" while watching or performing in the arts? What happens to you during these times?

2. Why do you think the arts continue to be devalued in some educational systems? What do you think is misunderstood by the people making the decisions to cut arts programs?

3. Are you a musician, visual artist, woodworker, gardener, writer, photographer, dancer? Perhaps your greatest artistic achievement has been making a ceramic vase or singing in a school chorus. What is it like for you when you are caught up in the Holy Ground of art? Can you explain it to a friend or a group?

4. "Just because you do something well doesn't mean it is your vocation." I cannot remember who said this, but I think it's an important statement. There are talented artists who have an entirely different vocation. How can you tell the difference between someone just "doing their job" and someone living vocationally?

Blessed and Blessing

*Thousands of candles can be lit from a single candle,
and the life of the candle will not be shortened. Happiness never
decreases by being shared.*

The Buddha[48]

Do What You Love, The Money Will Follow, written by Marsha Sinetar, hit the self-help book market in 1987. It is a good read about working with your innate gifts and doing the work that you love. The book is full of inspirational testimonies and much practical advice. The premise is a provocative and seductive idea, but it simply is not true. Think of all the brilliant musicians, artists, actors, writers, pastors, and teachers in the world who follow their bliss and bless us with their gifts, only to have to live paycheck to paycheck. Then there are others who are able to practice their art only because they are supported by a partner or benefactor. Some work full-time jobs to support themselves, and their bliss becomes their hobby. Many who do what they love live with no health insurance or retirement accounts.

The problem with Sinetar's thesis is that it links financial success to vocational success. There are fields of work where the two may go hand in hand. Technology, medical and pharmacological research, investments, professional sports, and some entrepreneurial endeavors come to mind. But for so many, what God calls them to, what becomes their life's work and offering, may have nothing to do with monetary success.

One of my best friends, Jan, lives in Manhattan. Her entire professional life has been devoted to children and families who live with disabilities. Immediately after graduating from college, she taught special education in the public schools. Then she started a private school for children with learning disabilities, worked as a learning disabilities consultant, was an adjunct professor at Furman University, and finally went on to get her doctorate in disability studies from an Ivy League school. There she wrote a dissertation that quickly received a book offer from an educational press. She now teaches at The City College of New York with the kind of passion and dedication that is the hallmark of great professors, and she is the director of their childhood education program. She's written another book and speaks all over the world on her passion—the perception and treatment of mothers of disabled children.

On a Saturday night in 2011, an adaptation of her dissertation debuted as a play performed at The City College of New York entitled *The M.O.M. Project: Mothers on Mothering: Narratives of Disability*. Just as the book that followed her dissertation was not her idea, this play was not her idea. An actor/playwright/director who knew of her work and dissertation had a vision of its becoming a play. So this theatre artist followed *her* passion—educational theatre—and turned the book into a play. Having seen that performance, a documentary filmmaker in attendance asked to interview Jan for her own project, a documentary on mothers and mothering. I imagine the energy playing out in this progression to be something like a candle lighting; someone lights my candle and I light the next person's candle and they light the candle next to them and soon we have a room glowing with light.

Jan will never be rich. There is no big money in education, no great return for writing a popular textbook and certainly none for saying yes to artists who are inspired by your work and want to share it with the world. Our culture's money structure does not, as a rule, particularly value teachers, children, mothers, or artists, and certainly we do not hold those with disabilities of any kind in great regard. What I know, however, is that my friend as a person, and the work to which she has given her life, have been a blessing beyond words to so many people. The joy of serving a passion that you believe in cannot be measured in dollars. The path she has followed, the journey to be true to her own life's story, has been a faithful path and it has blessed others infinitely.

Not surprisingly, by generously blessing others with her life's work, she is being blessed beyond measure. She feels fulfilled, there has been healing of some of her life's wounds, she is full of joy and has a sense of having mattered to the world. She has met and befriended talented and passionate people, and her calling is repeatedly affirmed. She is open to having her work take on new dimensions, and she is "just saying yes" to letting the energy take her work where it may. I am privileged to know others, many others, who live and work in the same way. By just saying yes to what is calling them, they become ordinary saints who are changing the world. Perhaps, dear Reader, you are one of them.

In the moment, my friend is inspiring me. By staying faithful to my call and therefore to God's call in my life, I can live in the knowledge that my work is a blessing and it will be blessed. Deeper still, and harder to say out loud, I can live with the confidence that, because I am blessed by God first, I am a blessing to others. We were created to become living sacraments, outward and visible signs of God's inward and spiritual grace. When we live out of that abundance, as my friend has, the blessings never end.

So don't do what you love because the money will follow. Do what you love because that love, that desire, was planted in you at your making. And when you live out of that place, whether living paycheck to paycheck or having more than enough financial success, you will be blessed and you will be a blessing. The cycle is infinite and its components cannot be separated: Blessedblessingblessedblessingblessedblessing . . . eternally.

DIGGING DEEPER

1. What do you love to do that would never be able to pay the bills? Does this make it any less valuable to you? To your friends? Your family? Your community?

2. How are you personally affected by what our world rewards with money and what it doesn't? Think about things you do that are rewarded with money and things that are rewarded in some other way. How do you respond to these differently?

3. What is the closest you have ever come to following your bliss and just watching the energy take on a life of its own? Write about it or tell about it in a group.

4. What are some ways you can do those things that feed your soul and give creative expression to your life? If you can't do them for a living, how can you do them?

Worth the Wait

"What makes the desert beautiful," said the little prince,
"is that somewhere it hides a well."
—Antoine de St. Exupéry[49]

"This is for you," the woman said as she handed my friend a crumpled up note and quickly walked away. After smoothing the scrap of paper open, he read it and looked at me with tears in his eyes. I read the note he handed me: "Two years ago I came to your church wounded and raw. I was at the lowest point in my life. You gave me hope. I will never forget you."

"Breathe it in," I said gently.

This doesn't happen very often to priests and others, like me, in the helping professions. A scrap of appreciation like that can make our year. Seriously. It can keep us focused on why we do what we do. It can help us continue to be faithful, even when the fruits of our labor seem hidden and we wonder if we're making a difference at all.

While we continued to eat and talk, I remembered the summer before my seventh-grade year. My family vacationed every July at a YMCA camp on Lake George, New York, called Silver Bay. For a week every summer, Lutheran families converged at this wonderful camp and enjoyed what for me was a magical time. The kids were free to do kid things and the adults did adult things. We met up only for meals and evening worship.

Pastor Ed was my favorite pastor. He played the guitar and had a clear, tenor voice. I loved to sing along with him and, even though I was still in elementary school, I paid attention when he preached. One night the sermon was called "The Waiting Game." I certainly didn't know why at the time, but this sermon touched me and has continued to be in my memory for forty years now.

What I remember hearing clearly that night is how we have to wait for God, and how things develop and grow in ways we cannot even imagine. On that long-ago night, Pastor Ed spoke of Abraham and Sarah waiting for a baby, Moses wandering around the desert, King David, Mary, and Jesus. At the ripe old age of twelve, I knew there was something about this sermon that was powerfully important. I don't know how, but in my core I must have known that I would need to learn how to wait.

We can't know now how the seeds of our efforts will affect people. We can't know how people will grow, how they will be tended to, pruned, fertilized, or watered. All we can do is live our lives faithfully, looking ahead, planting and tending the seeds we are called to plant and tend. We can only be who we are, live out of our very personal vocational calling, and The Holy Mystery will do the rest.

For me, and I believe for others, it takes a deep amount of discipline and faith to live life this way. The discipline comes in tending to the presence or seed of God within us. We do this by praying, reading, studying, and meditating. We do this by living in community and allowing ourselves to be accountable to others. We do this by paying attention to our inner lives through spiritual direction, dream work, creative outlets, and therapy. It takes faith to continue to allow the God-seed to grow, and then to help that growth manifest and take a shape in the world. We don't know if we will succeed or fail. We don't know if anything we do will matter. But we are called to do it anyway, and then to step back, let God be God, and watch what happens. We continue in the discipline so that we can faithfully respond to what happens next, and thus the cycle continues.

This summer I am spending time every day tending my plants. I am watering, fertilizing, deadheading, transplanting, pruning, picking, and spraying. I am praying over a few and singing to a couple of them. One even evoked a phrase from my lips that I heard my grandmother say one time: "Grow, dammit."

And then I stand back, wait, and see what they want to do. They have a life and a potential of their own, and when even one of them blooms into a full expression of who it is, I often feel a tear of gratitude.

Breathe it in, I tell myself. It was worth the wait.

Digging Deeper

1. How good are you at waiting? What in your life have you waited patiently for? Impatiently? Were they worth the wait?

2. Think about an experience, like the one the priest had in this story, when something you did or said was brought back to your attention at a much later date. What was that like for you?

3. We never know what kind of impact our living vocationally will have on others. But we can hope for things. What is your hope for how you might be impacting the world?

4. Right now, in the moment, what are you waiting for?

5. We live in a world where the ability to wait is not valued as much as it used to be. Often people get what they want quickly. What virtues do you think waiting helps form?

Epilogue

Dear Reader,

You are at the end of my book, and I want to thank you for taking the time to explore this process called transformation. You can never know where this process will take you. Sometimes it may feel like a step forward. Other times two steps back. Or maybe you will have times when you feel as if you are standing still. What I know is this. You are already on a journey, and that journey has no beginning and no end. Perhaps my book gave you the hunger and courage to step into a new phase of your journey. Perhaps it encouraged you during a difficult time, a time when you felt like you went two steps back. Perhaps it affirmed the wisdom of following the path you are already on. We all have our personal journey. But that is not enough. We must take ourselves into the world and journey together. Remember the infinity sign!

Framed and in my office are these words by Frederick Buechner:

> Listen to your life. See it for the fathomless mystery it is. In the boredom and pain of it, no less than in the excitement and gladness: touch, taste, smell your way to the holy and hidden heart of it, because in the last analysis all moments are key moments, and life itself is grace.[50]

This is really the essence of what I hope for all of us. That by paying attention, moment to moment, we will experience the holiness of life and the mystery of God, within ourselves and in the world. That by claiming these experiences of holiness and mystery, we will know life as abundant and infinite. And with this knowing, we then have the desire to fearlessly offer ourselves to the world.

Recommended Readings and Resources

This is a short list of some favorite books recommended for each of the five sections of this book. I have tried to include books that have not only been helpful to me, but ones that are consistently used by friends and colleagues on the journey. Some of these are classics. Some are new. I give them only as a place to start. There are many wonderful resources, so be open to finding the ones that are best for you.

Inner Work is God's Work

Au, Wilkie and Noreen Cannon. *Urgings of the Heart: A Spirituality of Integration.* New York: Paulist, 1995.

Brehoney, Janice. *Awakening at Midlife: Realizing Your Potential for Growth and Change.* New York: Riverhead Books, 1996.

Brown, Brené. *Daring Greatly: How the Courage to Be Vulnerable Transforms the Way We Live, Love, Parent, and Lead.* New York: Penguin Group, 2012.

Hart, Thomas. *Spiritual Quest: A Guide to the Changing Landscape.* Mahwah, NJ: Paulist Press, 1999.

Johnson, Robert. *Inner Work.* San Francisco: HarperSanFrancisco, 1986.

Johnson, Robert. *Owning Your Own Shadow.* San Francisco: HarperSanFrancisco, 1991.

Kelsey, Morton. *Dreams: A Way to Listen to God.* New York: Paulist Press, 1978.

May, Gerald. *Will and Spirit.* San Francisco: HarperSanFrancisco, 1982.

Holy Ground: Worship

Adams, William Seth. *Shaped by Images.* New York: Church Publishing Inc., 2000.

Benson, Robert. *Living Prayer.* New York: Putnam, 1998.

Benson, Robert. *Venite: A Book of Daily Prayer.* New York: Putnam, 2000.

Taylor, Barbara B. *An Altar in the World: A Geography of Faith.* New York: HarperCollins Publishers, 2009.

Wright, N.T. *For All God's Worth: True Worship and the Calling of the Church.* Grand Rapids, MI: William B. Eerdmans Publishing Company, 1994.

Holy Ground: Encounters

Bass, Dorothy. *Receiving the Day: Christian Practices for Opening the Gift of Time.* San Francisco: Jossey-Bass, 2000.

Chittister, Joan. *Wisdom Distilled from the Daily: Living the Rule of St. Benedict Today.* San Francisco: HarperSanFrancisco, 1990.

Newell, J. Philip. *Christ of the Celts: The Healing of Creation.* San Francisco: Jossey-Bass, 2008.

Norris, Kathleen. *Amazing Grace: A Vocabulary of Faith.* New York: Riverhead Books, 1998.

Norris, Kathleen. *The Quotidian Mysteries: Laundry, Liturgy, and "Women's Work."* New York: Paulist Press, 1998.

Rohr, Richard. *Everything Belongs: The Gift of Contemplative Prayer.* New York: Crossroads Publishing Company, 1999.

Rohr, Richard. *The Naked Now: Learning to See as the Mystics See.* New York: Crossroads Publishing Company, 2009.

Loafing with God

Dawn, Marva. *Keeping the Sabbath Wholly: Ceasing, Resting, Embracing, Feasting*. Grand Rapids, MI: William B. Eerdmans Publishing Company, 1989.

Edwards, Tilden. *Sabbath Time*. Nashville, TN: Upper Room Books, 1992.

Keating, Thomas. *Open Mind, Open Heart*. New York: Amity House, 1986.

Keating, Thomas. *Invitation to Love: The Way of Christian Contemplation*. New York: Continuum Publishing Company, 2003.

Kelly, Thomas. *A Testament of Devotion*. San Francisco: HarperSanFrancisco, 1941.

Kelsey, Morton. *The Other Side of Silence*. New York: Paulist Press, 1976.

Merton, Thomas. *A Seven Story Mountain*. New York: Harcourt Brace and Company, 1948.

Merton, Thomas. *What Is Contemplation?* Springfield, IL: Templegate Publishers, 1950.

Muller, Wayne. *Sabbath: Finding Rest, Renewal, and Delight in Our Busy Lives*. New York: Bantam, 1999.

Steere, Douglas. *Dimensions of Prayer: Cultivating a Relationship with God*. Nashville, TN: Upper Room Books, 1962.

Friends, Family, and Community

Buechner, Frederick. *Telling Secrets: A Memoir*. San Francisco: HarperSanFrancisco, 1991.

Ferrini, Paul. *The Twelve Steps of Forgiveness: A Practical Manual for Moving from Fear to Love*. Greenfield: Heartways Press, 1991.

Gallagher, Nora. *Practicing Resurrection: A Memoir of Work, Doubt, Discernment, and Moments of Grace*. New York: Alfred A. Knopf, 2003.

Gottman, John. *The Seven Principles that Make a Marriage Work*. New York: Three Rivers Press, 1999.

Nouwen, Henri. *The Prodigal Son: A Story of Homecoming*. New York: Doubleday, 1992.

O'Donohue, John. *Anam Cara: A Book of Celtic Wisdom*. New York: HarperCollins Publishers, 1997.

Palmer, Parker. *A Hidden Wholeness: The Journey Toward an Undivided Life*. San Francisco: Jossey-Bass, 2004.

Wuellner, Flora S. *Forgiveness, the Passionate Journey: Nine Steps of Forgiving Through Jesus' Beatitudes*. Nashville, TN: Upper Room Books, 2001.

Vocation

Buechner, Frederick. *Now and Then*. New York: HarperCollins Publishers, 1983.

Linn, Dennis, Matthew Linn, and Shelia Fabricant Linn. *Healing the Purpose of Your Life*. Mahwah, NJ: Paulist Press, 1999.

Moore, Thomas. *A Life at Work: The Joy of Discovering What You Were Born to Do*. New York: Doubleday Publishing Company, 2008.

Palmer, Parker. *Let Your Life Speak: Listening for the Voice of Vocation*. San Francisco: Jossey-Bass, 2000.

Palmer, Parker. *The Courage to Teach: Exploring the Inner Landscape of a Teacher's Life*. San Francisco: Jossey-Bass, 1998.

Placher, William C. *Callings: Twenty Centuries of Christian Wisdom on Vocation*. Grand Rapids, MI: William B. Eerdmans Publishing Company, 2005.

Poets to Accompany You on Your Spiritual Quest:

Mary Oliver

John O'Donohue

Danna Faulds

Rumi

Hafiz

David Whyte

T. S. Elliott

Thomas Merton

Teilhard de Chardin

Notes

1. David Whyte, "Start Close In," *River Flow: New and Selected Poems: 1984–2007* (Langely, WA: Many Rivers Press, 2007).

2. Peggy Van Antwarp Hill, private conversation.

3. Emily Brontë, *Wuthering Heights* (New York: W.W. Norton & Company, 2002 edition).

4. *Northern Exposure*: Season 2, Episode 2, "The Big Kiss."

5. Frank Honeycutt, *The Truth Shall Make You Odd: Speaking with Pastoral Integrity in Awkward Situations* (Grand Rapids: MI: Brazos Press, 2011).

6. Marilyn Ferguson, unsourced.

7. Words by F. Pratt Green, *The Hymnal 1982* (New York: The Church Pension Fund, 1985), hymn 424. Reprinted with permission by Church Publishing Incorporated.

8. Margaret Shepard, unsourced.

9. Agnes deMille, *Martha: The Life and Work of Martha Graham* (New York: Random House, 1991).

10. Anne Lamott, *Bird by Bird: Some Instructions on Writing and Life* (New York: Anchor Books, 1994).

11. George Herbert, *Jacula Prudentum #966*, 1651.

12. Samuel Rutherford, *Joshua Redivivus, or Three Hundred and fifty-two religious letters, Letter #167* (11th ed.; Glasgow: William Bell, 1796).

13. Stanley Hauerwaus and William Willimon, *Resident Aliens: A Provocative Assessment of Culture and Ministry for Those who Know Something is Wrong* (Nashville, TN: Abingdon Press, 1989).

14. Fyodor Dostoevsky, *The Idiot*, trans. Richard Pevear (New York: Vintage Press, 2001 edition).

15. Madeleine L'Engle, *Walking on Water: Reflections on Faith and Art* (Wheaton, IL: Harold Shaw Publishers,1980).

16. Richard Rohr, *Falling Upward: A Spirituality for the Two Halves of Life* (San Francisco: Jossey-Bass, 2011).

17. Words by F. Pratt Green, *The Hymnal 1982* (New York: The Church Pension Fund, 1985), hymn 424. Reprinted with permission by Church Publishing Incorporated.

18. Aldous Huxley, unsourced.

19. Hafiz, "Where is the Door to the Tavern?," in *The Gift: Poems by Hafiz, the Great Spiritual Master*, trans. Daniel Ladinsky (New York: Penguin Group,1999).

20. Hafiz, "Your Mother and My Mother," in *The Gift: Poems by Hafiz, the Great Spiritual Master*, trans. Daniel Ladinsky (New York: Penguin Group,1999).

21. Mary Oliver, *Low Tide, Amicus Journal*, Winter, 34 2001.

22. Mary Oliver, "Snow Geese," in *Why I Wake Early: New Poems* (Boston: Beacon Press, 2004).

23. Richard Rohr and John Feister, *Radical Grace: Daily Meditations* (Cincinnati, OH: St. Anthony Messenger Press,1995).

24. Hafiz, "Today," in *The Gift: Poems by Hafiz, the Great Spiritual Master*. Trans. Daniel Ladinsky (New York: Penguin Group, 1999).

25. Wayne Mueller, *How, Then Shall We Live? Four Simple Questions that Reveal the Beauty and Meaning of Our Lives* (New York: Bantam Press, 1996).

26. Washington Irving, unsourced.

27. Frank Honeycutt, *The Truth Shall Make You Odd: Speaking with Pastoral Integrity in Awkward Situations* (Grand Rapids, MI: Brazos Press, 2011).

28. William Blake, "The Marriage of Heaven and Hell," in *Blake's Poetry and Designs*, Mary Lynn Johnson and John E. Grant eds. (New York: Norton, 1979).

29. Danna Faulds, "Go In and In," in *Go In and In: Poems from the Heart of Yoga* (Kearsey, NE: Morris Press, 2002).

30. Carl G. Jung, *Modern Man in Search of a Soul* (Oxford, England: Routledge Classics, 2001 edition).

31. Morton Kelsey, *The Other Side of Silence* (Mahwah, NJ: Paulist Press, 1995).

32. Macrina Wiederkehr, "Prayer of the Empty Water Jar," in *Seasons of Your Heart: Prayers and Reflections* (New York: HarperCollinsPublishers, 1991).

33. Albert Blackwell, *The Sacred In Music* (Louisville, KY: Westminster John Knox, 1999).

34. Anne Lamott, *Traveling Mercies: Some Thoughts on Faith* (New York: First Anchor, 2000).

35. Joanna Macy, *www.joannamacy.net* (accessed March 2013).

36. Antoine de St. Exupéry, "Generation to Generation," unsourced.

37. Tom Conlon, "Leaning," in *Country Dog, City Boy* (New York: Top Five Music, Tom Conlon Music, 2001).

38. Malidoma Somé in a speech at Kanuga Camp and Conference Center, 2001.

39. Brené Brown, from a lecture given at Furman University, Greenville, SC, February 2013.

40. Carl Whitaker, from a lecture given at a South Carolina Association of Marriage and Family Therapy conference, sometime in the 1980s.

41. Klingsporn, Gary W. (ed.). *The Library of Distinctive Sermons, Volume 5* (Colorado Springs: Multnomah Books, 1997).

The line "the love that lies beneath the woe" was adapted from Melville's *Moby Dick* by Carlyle Marney, who made use of it in a sermon preached more than thirty years ago. Reference to the sermon, "When Wisdom Flirts with Madness," is found in John Carey, *Carlyle Marney: A Pilgrim's Progress* (Macon, GA: Mercer University Press, 1980), 125.

42. Elizabeth O'Connor, *Journey Inward, Journey Outward* (New York: Harper & Row, 1975).

43. Kahlil Gibran, "On Children," in *The Prophet* (New York: Alfred Knopf Publishers, 1973).

44. Dennis Merritt Jones, *The Art of Uncertainty: How to Live in the Mystery of Life and Love It* (New York: Tarcher/Penguin, 2011).

45. Frederick Buechner, *Wishful Thinking: A Theological ABC* (New York: Harper & Row, 1973).

46. Hafiz, "A Hard Decree," in *The Gift: Poems by Hafiz, the Great Spiritual Master*, trans. Daniel Ladinsky (New York: Penguin Group, 1999).

47. Anita Robertson, unsourced.

48. The Buddha, unsourced.

49. Antoine de St. Exupéry, *The Little Prince* (Hertfordshire, Great Britian: Wordsworth Editions Limited, 1995 edition).

50. Frederick Buechner, *Now and Then* (San Francisco: Harper & Row. 1983).